Indian & White

Every Indian is not an orator, but they are all adepts at "sounding"—that is, weighing and gauging the influences that sway the person they are addressing, with a view at addressing all their efforts to the weakest point. Their preliminary talk is all aimed at this, and what follows is an appeal, an argument, or a threat, as they have decided the occasion requires. I have watched this process over and over again, and wondered at it as often; first he will try to frighten you, and, if he finds this is not working, will gradually change his tone until he has found the feeling you will respond to.

ROBERT JEFFERSON
Fifty Years on the Saskatchewan

Indian & White

*Self-Image and Interaction
in a Canadian Plains Community*

NIELS WINTHER BRAROE

Stanford University Press, Stanford, California

Stanford University Press
Stanford, California
© 1975 by the Board of Trustees of the
Leland Stanford Junior University
Printed in the United States of America
Cloth ISBN 0-8047-0877-0   Paper ISBN 0-8047-1028-7
Original edition 1975
Last figure below indicates year of this printing:
88 87 86 85 84 83 82 81 80 79

Original edition published with the assistance
of the Andrew W. Mellon Foundation

To Pop, Flip, and Little Peter

Acknowledgments

IT HAS BEEN eleven years since I first met the people of Short Grass—a long time, just as I ought to have finished this book a long time ago. By now, there are many to thank.

I owe my introduction to anthropology to the late Jules Henry, who first communicated to me the intense excitement of discovery, and the rewards of cultivating curiosity even when there are no easy answers. The encouragement (and occasional prodding) of Edward M. Bruner kept me in graduate school, though at times it was touch and go, and much of my view of interethnic relations comes from contact with him. Gregory P. Stone first introduced me to the perspective of symbolic interactionism, in ways that only a great teacher can manage.

Joseph B. Casagrande and Philip E. Leis read the entire manuscript and offered many valuable suggestions. My friend and colleague George L. Hicks suffered through numberless hours of my talk about cowboys and Indians, and read the original draft page by page as it came off the typewriter. He was both patient and helpful. Norman K. Denzin read an earlier draft of the book, and I have made numerous revisions as a result of his pointing out to me confused or confusing passages.

Eva Braroe accompanied me to Short Grass for part of my 1966–67 stay, and again briefly visited there in the summer of 1971. Even though she had other things to do, she joined me in work on the Cree language (in which I became only minimally competent), and contributed sensitive observations about the daily lives of Indians and Whites. At times when I felt discouraged about the entire project, her encouragement helped me push on.

I wish also to express my gratitude to the Department of Anthropology at Brown University, and especially to its chairman, Philip E. Leis, for the patience and indulgence extended to me while I wrote. My students have been sympathetic, too, and many of the ideas and hunches gained from them are reflected in the following pages. I could not have asked for a more congenial atmosphere in which to work.

I find it difficult to express my indebtedness to the Indians of Short Grass. Regrettably, I cannot acknowledge individuals or the community itself by name if I am to preserve its residents' anonymity. My gratitude to them is not simply for providing the material for this study, but also for receiving me into their community, for putting up with my foibles, and for giving me their affection, friendship, and trust. They did not have to do this, but acted out of a disposition toward gentleness and good humor that was evidenced daily. This book is a small down payment on my debt to them.

N.W.B.

Copenhagen, July 1974

Contents

Eight pages of photographs follow p. 110

PART ONE

Preliminaries

ONE   A Problem and a Wedge

THIS STUDY was begun as an enquiry into the process of self-identification among the people of Short Grass, a small Canadian Prairie community, and especially among the Cree Indians of the region. The task was to discover what conceptions Indians hold of their social selves in various situations and how these conceptions are formed and modified. As time passed, one question took on crucial significance: in the circumstance of being moral outcasts vis-à-vis White people, how do Indians attempt to sustain a morally defensible self-image? We must assume that this essential task confronts all humans to some degree, in that all must create for themselves the self-image of persons of competence, persons who deserve respect. The problem becomes even more complex if we require that esteem must come both from oneself and from others, since these two sources are not independent of one another. And this condition is especially problematical for persons whose moral worth is routinely challenged or denied by others.

Let me explain. In Short Grass, as in every community, there are existing standards and ideals that provide a measure for the achievements and performances of all people. To be sure, no individual completely embodies all the desirable qualities, and some people are always more admired than others. In Short Grass, Whites attempt to project and defend images of themselves as competent, worthy, and unblemished, and they frequently do this at the implicit (and sometimes explicit) expense of Indians. Indians thus have to face the more or less continual condemnation of their White neighbors in nearly all spheres of human activity: in work and economic pursuits, in recreational and leisure activities, and in family and public life. It seems that little of the Indians' observed behavior—and much that is not observed but is traditionally ascribed to them—escapes critical comment by Whites.

One hears, for example, that doctors and nurses do not like to treat Indians because of their filthy habits. In one case, I was told that an Indian woman who had taken whiskey to deaden a toothache was thrown out of a dentist's office because the doctor refused to care for an Indian who was "liquored up." It is also rumored that Indians have "bad morals" sexually, and that many of them are afflicted with venereal disease. One White woman told me that when Indians return from a distant Sun Dance or powwow, VD assumes epidemic proportions on the Short Grass reserve, as though the travelers had participated in an extended orgy. Whites suppose that violence and even murder are commonplace on the reserve, making it a place for respectable people to stay away from.

Above all, Indians are believed to lack integrity and honesty. A local lawyer once explained to me that Indians are rarely called to testify at court trials because "you can't trust 'em as far as you can throw 'em . . . and the judge just has to assume that they're lying." Even when an Indian testifies on his own behalf, as in one case I observed, a similar attitude prevails. An Indian man and woman had been arrested while sleeping in an old car in which there was an opened bottle of wine (it is illegal to have an open bottle in one's car). In court, the Indian man argued that the liquor was not his: he did not know it was there, and had he known of its existence, he and his companion would certainly have drunk it. The magistrate agreed that no Indian would leave a bottle half consumed, and dismissed the case.

The list of indictments is almost endless. Indians are regarded as totally lacking in industry, self-sufficiency, reliability, and punctuality. And in making such pronouncements, Whites characteristically begin their remarks with, "Of course, I'm not prejudiced, but. . . ." The Indians of Short Grass are quite aware that these judgments are made about them in the White community. One elderly Indian, for example, showed me an old clipping from the local newspaper, which he had carried in his wallet for several years. It was a letter to the editor from a town resident, who blamed a group of young Indians for vandalism on his property and then went on to attack Indians in general in extremely derogatory terms. Its contents were still vigorously resented by Indians, and the old man remarked to me: "It don't make any difference, whenever one of us does somethin' they don't like, they blame us all as a bunch."

Whites commonly tell Indians directly that they may not borrow some small sum of money asked for because they cannot be trusted to repay it; they are refused credit in local stores; and Indian agents periodically discontinue cash welfare payments with the express intent of curtailing liquor expenditures, instead depositing the funds in town general stores where Indians may draw food and clothing. Low regard for Indians is expressed directly and indirectly in innumerable ways. For example, Whites will "take liberties" with Indians they would not take with other Whites, and it is not uncommon to hear White men engage in boisterous sexual banter with Indian women, in marked contrast to the gallant chivalry they display toward White women. One (male) Indian concluded: "They treat us like cattle here. . . . Worse even; they care more about their lousy cows than they do about us. They think they're so good, and we're nothin'. It don't matter what kind of person you are; as long as you got some color on you, you're dirt."

Short Grass Whites, of course, must also acquire morally defensible images of self. In the context of standards by which persons' worth and achievements are measured, Whites attempt to project and have validated self-images that are fine and worthy. The different problems of Indians and Whites in realizing such identities are largely a result of prevailing social stratification arrangements—that is, of the two groups' relative positions in the social hierarchy. Consequently, a recurrent problem in this book is the manner in which Indians and Whites represent moral "threats" to one another, and how each group deals with these threats. Greater attention will be given to the Indians' strategies, since the problem for them, as persons lacking community respectability, is a more pressing one.

The Meeting of Cultures

This study fits into, but departs from, the field of anthropological research that deals with "culture contact" or "acculturation." The voluminous literature on the subject—much of it dealing with North American Indian groups—touches on a wide range of topics. In fact, it is this multiplicity of problems, methods, and theoretical perspectives that makes it difficult to briefly and accurately characterize the field. There have been studies of linguistic change and bilingualism, of Indian children in White-run schools, of cultural disorganization, of the sometimes violent response by Indians to encroaching White society, and of "nativistic" religious movements that have developed among Indian groups confronted with threats to their cultural integrity and physical existence. Many of these works have been quite specialized or technical in nature, concerning such areas as ecological and technological change, shifts in music and other art forms, and the modification of such specific aspects of social structure as kinship terminology or political organization. Still others have sought for comparative generalizations, attempting to explain why the course of historic events has been different for various tribes, why some tribes seem to have accommodated Western society with greater ease than others, or why Indian groups today show such a wide range in degree of acculturation. Indians have also been compared with other ethnic groups—for example, in their characteristic responses to life in the cities.

Despite great variation in their special interests, most of these investigations fall into one of two broad categories. First, certain writers have examined the conjunctive relations of various societies and cultures and have delineated the resulting structural modifications. Generally, such studies take a view of culture and society that does not include the variety of ways these are experienced by individuals. Instead, emphasis is placed on other units of analysis, such as institutions, ecological phenomena, and abstract value codes. All of these, in turn, are believed to be linked together in ordered social or cultural "systems." By considering the differences between two juxtaposed systems, and the structural changes produced in each system by contact, writers have endeavored to isolate various "processes" of change. Linton (1940: 503) was among the first to identify different kinds of change, distinguishing "directed," "enforced," and "fusional" acculturation.

A second approach to acculturation is more "psychologically" oriented, in that it attempts to detect transformations in individual cognitive and emotional experience. A. I. Hallowell, a respected student of these phenomena, has defined the scope of this approach (1955: 307–8):

We know that if any people undergo changes in their mode of life eventuating in new or varied culture patterns this implies some readjustment in the habits, attitudes, and goals of the individuals concerned, that such processes of readjustment have to be motivated, and that learning is involved. These are the most obvious psychological events that any process of acculturation implies. . . . But there is a further question that invites inquiry. Instead of being concerned with the goals and motivations of individuals which *lead* to the acceptance of new cultural items . . . we are now confronted with the psychological *depth* of the readjustments—with the cumulative psychological effects which acceptance may bring about in a given population over a period of time.

Students have consequently looked both for the personal characteristics that dispose individuals to accept or reject aspects of alien cultures and for the consequences of this acceptance/rejection for people as well as for abstract cultures or societies. There seems to be a consensus that the transitional stage—when a person is neither fully Indian nor fully White—is necessarily one of stress, personal disorganization, and behavioral pathogenesis.[1] To be "between two worlds" forces individuals into conflicts of choice and produces casualties among those who cannot embrace either the

---

[1] Margaret Mead's 1932 monograph on "Antler" Indians was concerned with these problems, especially as they were experienced by women. More recently, Jessor et al. (1968), Graves (1967), Chance (1965), and Opler (1959) have dealt with related questions, especially that of deviance.

old or the new ways exclusively (see Spindler and Goldschmidt, 1952: 80). The frequently observed and much discussed problem of alcoholism in many Indian groups is a good example of this type of research (Honigman and Honigman, 1944; Lemert, 1954).

The focus and approach of this study are somewhat different: it seeks not only to bridge the two orientations so far outlined, but to deal with problems that neither has successfully confronted.[2]

The "structural" studies have given us a typology of acculturative processes—for example, "reactive adaptation" and "progressive adjustment" (SSRC, 1954: 487)—in before-and-after examinations of cultures in contact (if such phenomena can indeed be seen to occur). But they have not told us how these processes work, that is, how individuals come to act in ways such that their acts cumulatively bring about or retard institutional and cultural change. Here, I shall concentrate on showing how people respond in their daily lives to the perceived facts of their social existence. More specifically, I wish to describe how Indians, in particular, interpret circumstances and adapt to them, especially as their acts work to define them as Indians. This is not a passive process, and the behavior of both Indians and Whites as individuals has profound implications for the stability or change of the larger community.

The "psychological" studies have produced insight into the problems and stresses experienced by acculturating individuals, but they have not described the specific cultural contexts in which these experiences take place. They have given us typologies of persons—nativistic or traditional, transitional or marginal, as-

[2] Many studies, of course, have attempted to deal with both of the dimensions outlined here. The SSRC programmatic treatment of acculturation (1954), for example, calls for the study of "personality and acculturation" (albeit in an appendix, pp. 993–94) as well as the structural dimensions of the acculturation process. Other well-known reports have attempted to relate personality changes to social and cultural variables in a systematic manner; see Bruner (1956), Spindler and Goldschmidt (1952), and McFee (1968) as examples. One writer (Murphy, 1964) has suggested that we drop the term acculturation from our lexicon altogether, claiming that it is not a process of change qualitatively different from others, and that it rests on erroneous assumptions regarding the isolation and autonomy of human societies.

similated or acculturated—but they have not told us how persons interact with one another, or how cultural norms and values are implicated in these interactions.[3] My task will include describing in detail how certain cultural values, Indian and White, are directly implicated in substantive and symbolic transactions between the two groups. For all participants, these values are more than guidelines for, or goals of, behavior; they also provide a symbolic means of presenting, evaluating, and defining the self. And cultural values are employed (differently) by the two groups to explain their perceptions of the state of the social universe.

Finally, it appears that neither the structural nor the psychological approach, or any combination of the two, has satisfactorily treated a problem of increasing significance: the persistence of what has been called "ethnic identity." Nearly twenty years ago, Hallowell observed this among the Ojibwa, without being able to explain it (1955: 351):

'Thus even the highly acculturated Indians at Flambeau are still Ojibwa in a psychological sense, whatever their clothes, their houses, or their occupations, whether they speak English or not, or regardless of race mixture. While culturally speaking they appear like "whites" in many respects, there is no evidence at all of a fundamental psychological transformation.

It appears that a great many cultural trappings, even language, can be lost or discarded with no concurrent loss of "Indianness." This obviously contradicts some previous assumptions about the unitary relationship of culture and personality, however defined.[4]

[3] There are many psychologically oriented acculturation studies that come close to doing this but fail for various reasons. A common procedure is to construct a typology of individuals based on extent of acculturation (often determined by projective test data), and then to link the selected differences to "external" factors such as personal history, education, or other means of access to White society (see Spindler and Goldschmidt, 1952; Spindler and Spindler, 1965). What is lacking is a description and analysis of the interactional content of behavior in its various settings. One consequence of this is that certain kinds of questions do not get asked: for example, how is it that Indians act like Indians in some situations and like Whites in others?

[4] Glaser and Moynihan (1963) have observed that even among the ethnic groups of New York City the "melting pot" expectation has not been borne out —that ethnic differences remain a significant factor in urban life.

Joan Ablon, in a study of Indians in the San Francisco Bay Area, concludes (1964: 303):

> The adjustments most Indians make in learning the cues for living successfully in the white world seem to be superficial to their established basic personality structures. Such basic qualities of Indianness—as Indian identity and continuing belief in early teachings and values—are strongly resistant to change.

The source of this resistance, and its outward expression, are the topics of this study. The avowed intention of the Indian Affairs Branch (IAB) of the Canadian government, and that of White community leaders, has been to facilitate the assimilation of Canadian Indians to White culture. Short Grass Indians no longer live in tepees, or even log houses. They wear the same Western-style clothing as their White neighbors, and almost all speak English. They have learned to manipulate White tools and have adopted many White forms of entertainment and recreation. No longer hunters and trappers, they now rely entirely on the White economy for their livelihood. But with all this, their sense of distinctiveness as Indians seems as strong as ever. In what follows, I will look for the source of this feeling not only in the structure of community social and cultural relations, but in the mundane interactions of individual Indians and Whites, and in the kinds of situations that provide the context of these interactions.

The theoretical perspective underlying this study is a kind of social psychology cumbersomely termed symbolic interactionism; and Chapter 2 offers a brief discussion of this orientation and some of its core concepts, together with an account of my own field research and my place as an observer in Short Grass. Chapters 3 and 4 describe the community itself, the aboriginal Indian way of life, and the historical events that attended White settlement of the area.

In Part Two I shall examine in some detail aspects of the day-to-day interaction between Indians and Whites. Chapter 5 discusses rules of etiquette and personal comportment, both diffuse and specific, and the various ways Indians are seen by Whites as breaking these rules. This is presented to give insight into the "profane" character of the social selves of Indians—profane, that is, in the judgment of Whites. The next three chapters discuss various adaptive strategies that Short Grass Indians have adopted in dealing with their profaneness. This is not a uniform or entirely consistent adaptation: at times, Indians behave as if they desire acceptance by Whites and assimilation into White society, and at other times as if they do not. When alienation is evident, it may be expressed either by withdrawal or by a frontal, exploitative attack on White institutions and conventions. All these stances, however, may be seen as the effort of a profane category of persons to salvage a measure of self-esteem. Finally, Chapter 9 discusses the process of acculturation in what amounts to a dual moral universe and the usefulness of the symbolic-interactionism perspective in understanding this process.

One last point. In this study I have used pseudonyms and have attempted to disguise the actual location of Short Grass. I have done this less to "protect" the community from the outside than to guard various members of the community from embarrassment, as I promised many informants I would. An assiduous detective, from internal evidence, could perhaps correctly identify the community, but not, in my opinion, to any useful purpose.

TWO Methods and Theories

AN ANTHROPOLOGIST sets himself no simple task when he goes into the field. As Stanley Diamond says (1964: xv),

In conceptualizing a primitive society, he interprets signs and symbols by exchanging places with the actors in the system under study. The mere cataloging or even systematic linking of institutions and artifacts is meaningless unless the effort to reproduce the social consciousness, the cultural being of the people who live and produce in their modality, is made.

Malinowski, too, warned that the final goal is "to grasp the native's point of view, his relation to life, to realize *his* vision of *his* world. We have to study man, and we must study what concerns him most intimately, that is, the hold which life has upon him" (1922: 25).

I carried these warnings with me the first time I set foot in Short Grass, and later progressed in my work to the degree that I could forget them, or at least forget the awkward self-consciousness they can produce. I took with me all the sources of malaise that I suppose many students do, especially the yearning to do "good fieldwork" in order to please my professors (and myself). Things went best, I think, when all of this was put aside and I simply traveled with my friends, as Indians put it. They taught me how.

This does not mean that I was free of self-consciousness, or ever completely comfortable, for there is a kind of tension or contradiction built into fieldwork that cannot be escaped. One participates in the daily lives of one's informants, but always with an eye to the data, to what is going to be recorded in one's notes. I can convey this mixture of involvement and detachment best, I think, with an excerpt from a letter written to my wife in the summer of 1971:

About 7 this evening I returned from Grace's funeral, which lasted something over 24 hours, during which I had maybe an hour's rest sitting on the floor. It was very draining. The whole thing was very moving, very dignified and beautiful.

We brought her home and opened the box she was in. Charlie [her husband] sat the whole night on the floor at the head, and after a short period of weeping explanation of how she died, we spent the rest of the evening talking and smoking (men on one side of the room, women on the other). The talk was about trivial things, telling of stories, and even some quiet laughter. The story about how Wilbert and I got beat up at Calgary, about so and so being thrown off a horse, about a wallet Charlie once found with some money in it (which he returned). When there was a pause, Charlie would say to someone (or to me), "Have you got a story to tell us?" Always, some people would be awake and some asleep. Cigarettes, tea, and food were passed about all night. We—Charlie, Grace, and the rest of us—were just having a very nice visit.

About 11 A.M. this morning, after people had returned home from other reserves, and the relatives from far away who had been summoned arrived, the body was prepared. Grace's face was painted brightly, she was dressed in a beautiful red fringed deerskin shawl with beadwork, a red-and-white headband with two eagle feathers sticking downward across her cheek, a red-and-white bead necklace, and white doeskin moccasins. Various small objects were placed in the box with her: a small plate, sweet grass, tobacco, and so on. Charlie, Joe, and a lady from Rocky Mountain House I did not know performed all of this while we watched, very lovingly and gently. During this time, the crying or wailing began. . . . I do not know what to call it, but people would break out into a kind of crying that was more like singing without words. But this was never loud or hysterical. There were prayers from Neminas and another guy, people filed past Grace, knelt on the floor and kissed or touched her lightly (this happened several times later in different contexts).

I was doing okay until the second or third time I heard Charlie's weeping, and then the dam burst and I flooded tears copiously. But I did so quietly, I think. It was strange that this happened then, and I know that I cried for somewhat different reasons than others, because there were other occasions when tears were not appropriate, and I had to hold them back.

I had been appointed by Gordon to help dig the grave, but at the last

minute Lawrence and I were dispatched to town to pick up some stragglers. (It is also significant, I think, that no specific person was in charge
of the entire funeral. Of course, old John and his wife were prominent,
as were Charlie, Neminas, and others. But everybody knew what to do
when; various persons assumed the tasks that needed doing, and even I
did not need too much guidance.)

We took her to the hills in a caravan of trucks and cars. Way up on
top, in a secluded place in the bush where I had never been before. It
was very green and lush with wild roses, a small sort of sunflower, and
other blooms I do not know the names of. There was more to be done
ceremonially, prayers, last touches, wailing, and lowering into the earth.
She was not covered directly, but over the hole were placed poplar logs
and, in turn, over this were placed blankets (including your green blanket
I brought with me). The dirt from the excavation was heaped over this.
Each of the men took turns with a shovel.

At the end, everyone turned and walked away in utter silence, no one
looking back. It was all done. There were quite a few of us—about a
hundred adults, I counted. I had seen a relatively fresh grave which must
have been Abel's. More (inappropriate) tears then. We returned to Gordon's place for a ritually communal "feast."

I shall have to spend all day tomorrow writing down all of the things
I saw, and there's the rub. All during this, while I kept making mental
notes of how long this or that phase took, of who did what, which objects
were involved, what the general ethos seemed to be at various points,
and so on, I could not help feeling how horrible this was. I was witness
and even to a little extent part of a very moving community grief and
coming-together, and at the same time I coldly collected the old ethnographic data. Hang in there, Niels. *They* took my presence to reflect my
commitment to the community and my feeling for it (my tears *were* real
ones), but behind my somber visage the data were being recorded all the
same. What the hell kind of business is this?[1]

As Denzin remarks (1970: 132–43), every researcher has his personal style, which has to modify what he sees and records. We sometimes get very good descriptions of this field conduct, as in Rosalie
Wax's account of her experiences (1971). I want to take some space
now to give the reader an idea of my own approach.

I spent a total of nearly two years in Short Grass, spread over

---

[1] Unless otherwise indicated, quoted matter in this study is derived from my
field notes, from letters in my possession, or from my own reconstructions of
conversations.

nearly a decade: a first visit in the summer of 1963, a longer stay during 1966–67, and a brief follow-up in the summer of 1971. At the beginning of my first stay, I had no more specific intention than a vague investigation of "Indian-White relations." I was simply doing the summer fieldwork required of fledgling anthropologists, and I had no plans to return to Short Grass.

On my first day in town I was fortunate enough to meet a rancher who lived only a mile from the Indian reserve. Abashed at his immediate invitation to put up at his place (a generosity I later learned was typical of people there), I nevertheless accepted. I was housed, and fed, and even loaned a horse to get to the reserve daily. Any sort of payment was refused, except that I was allowed to help with the ranching chores—not, I suspect, for the material assistance afforded as much as for the comic relief supplied by the sight of a city boy trying to heave a bale of hay or brand a calf. I learned much from this man and his family. My role, I soon discovered, was fixed by them as that of college student on summer vacation, not that of serious anthropologist (a word never encountered in Short Grass). I was kept busy the first couple of weeks just trying to straighten out my relationship with that goddamned horse. I never really did, though I did not confess that to my hosts.

I soon began to meet members of the nearby Indian band, who tolerated my intrusion graciously. I often went to the saloon in town to drink beer with young Indian men of my age, and we soon began to find things in common to talk about. Deciding that I did not want to become identified by Indians exclusively with the local Whites, I left the ranch and took up irregular residence on the reserve, staying with various families with whom I had become acquainted. Since I had no car, I depended on Indians, ranchers, and the reserve schoolteacher for transportation. My mobility was limited and unpredictable, and I could not always know in advance where I would spent the night—sometimes on the reserve, sometimes in a hotel room in town.

Because of my transportation difficulties, and because during so short a visit I had necessarily remained a stranger in Short Grass, I returned to the University with notes that were no more than impressions, although I had been able to interview a number of Indians and Whites and had collected kinship data and life histories material from both. I blush now at my naiveté that summer. I had, for example prepared a mimeoed checklist to inventory each Indian household interviewed, and had included an exhaustive set of categories—age, make, and date of acquisition of refrigerator, similar data for other appliances, and so on. The whole thing became scratch paper when I discovered that there was no electricity on the reserve. Similarly, my attempt at a precise household census was inevitably doomed, given the great mobility of Indians between households and even between reserves (especially in the summer months). Before going to Short Grass I assumed that there would be virtually nothing left of traditional culture; and therefore I did not bother to read the available ethnographic accounts of the Plains Cree, expecting to look through them later at my leisure. Consequently, I missed the significance of all sorts of things that did happen that summer, which took place before my eyes but went unremarked because I had no idea that anything significant was happening.

When I returned to Short Grass several years later, I had been awarded research funds to study "personal identity and culture change." This time my wife accompanied me, and we rented a small house in town for the winter. A few Indians had elected to live in town during cold weather, and in fairly formal sessions with them my wife (an accomplished linguist) and I began eliciting data on Cree language and kinship terminology. It often happened that Indians who were marooned in town by the weather stayed with us, and that one or both of us stayed on the reserve for the same reason. In the spring my wife returned to Sweden because of illness in her family, and at this time I moved onto the reserve. Rather than place additional strain on already crowded Indian households, and in order to have privacy for making notes, I lived in a tent.

The fact that I had been to Short Grass before helped to dispel much of the suspicion usually met by newcomers and permitted me to take up friendships begun during my previous visit. My wife's and my interest in Indian language and in the "old days" served as an initial definition of our role there, for both Indians and Whites: we were "college teachers" who had come to find out about local traditions (I was asked, for example, to write the history of a saddle and roping club). During all this, we were involved in a wide range of activities with both Indians and Whites. I helped Indian families cut and prepare fenceposts for sale, and assisted Indians and Whites in tending cattle and putting up winter hay. With varying frequency, I participated in nearly all the tasks essential to daily life on the reserve: shopping, hauling water and firewood, fixing cars and trucks, repairing fences, washing clothes, and preparing food. Some things, like picking berries and searching through the railway yards for pieces of coal, were seasonal. Others took place rarely or only once during this year: helping an Indian family rebuild their house, working with ranchers at calving and branding time, and working with Indians and Whites to repair the local stampede (rodeo) grounds in preparation for the annual celebration.

On the reserve, my wife and I joined in various religious events, the most significant of which was the Sun Dance. The preparations for this four-day observance were spread out over about six months, and when the time came we pitched our tent in an assigned spot in the camp circle during the ceremony. My wife, in a costume the other women had shown her how to make, took her place on the women's side of the Sun Dance lodge, where she danced in place with the rest. My part was that of drummer and singer, though my skill at the latter was negligible. We made pledges of thirsting and fasting, and offered cloth and tobacco to the spirits. There were no other Whites present, although there were visitors from other Indian communities.

With groups of Short Grass Indians we traveled to other Sun Dances, both in the United States and several hundred miles to the east in Canada. At these, as was the custom, we sat with the guests. These were larger, more elaborate affairs, usually attended by White tourists and spectators. At one, I drifted into the poker tent and soon became the only White player. An Indian companion had loaned me some of his "medicine" for luck, but the evening was financially disastrous nonetheless. Short Grass Indians, like the people of many Plains tribes, are avid and spontaneous travelers, and we accompanied them on many other trips—to powwows, to stampedes, and on shopping expeditions to the nearest small city. The longest of these forays lasted about a week, and sometimes several carloads made the journey.

Casual but more or less organized recreation is likely to take place at almost any time on the reserve, and we were not excluded from these events. On the spur of the moment, someone might organize a softball game, a communal sing, or a hand game. Birthday parties for children always attracted many adults (soda pop and cake for the former, wine for the latter). These were all times when people came together to "do something," but there were endless hours spent in leisurely chatting and gossiping, talking about recent events or happenings yet to take place.

To supplement this adventitiously collected information, I conducted more focused interviews. Several life histories were tape-recorded, as well as myths, origin legends, Windigo stories, and the like, related by elders in the band. I also spent a great deal of time, especially in the early part of my work, collecting genealogies and kinship data (the terminology of kinship did not differ significantly from the precontact system reported by Mandelbaum thirty years earlier). These formal data, however, were only a small part of all that I discovered. This was intentional. From my previous visit, I had learned that Indians would not respond readily to direct questioning, and that when they did so the answers were usually evasive; hence it seemed that questionnaires and other "structured" procedures would yield very little meaningful information. I decided that it would be more profitable to rely on being present and taking information as it was offered, saving my questions for conversational contexts in which they were appropriate. It was not possible to make notes at any scheduled time, such as every night before retiring. Instead, I used whatever time I had alone to record what I had been told or had observed. I did, however, carry a small pocket notebook so that I could jot down things shortly after they occurred.

Our relations with members of the White community changed considerably during this stay. At first, we were welcomed into local affairs, and were invited to parties and dances held by the Chamber of Commerce, as well as to private dinner parties, at which the conversation usually concerned Indians. I was able to discuss with community leaders and numerous local government representatives special facets of the "Indian problem" such as health and sanitation, medical care, and the legal and economic aspects of Indian citizenship. Over time, however, these relations cooled, for a number of reasons.

To begin with, although I did once speak to a group of school-teachers about what seemed to me the drawbacks in providing White education for Indians, I was generally reluctant to provide local Whites with information about the reserve community; and I declined when asked to participate in several paternalistic schemes to "help out our own Indians." The Whites of Short Grass must soon have concluded that I was not going to provide the kind of wedge into the reserve community that they seemed to desire. As I was increasingly seen in company with Indians, especially in the pubs and in the context of other activities that met with White disapproval, my purposes for being in Short Grass, and also my loyalties, were in doubt. After the first three months or so fewer "respectable" Whites called at our house, probably because Indians were likely to be found there. In the spring, our landlord demanded that we vacate his house, saying he did not want it to become "a hangout for a bunch of savages."

It should be mentioned that the Whites who became most reserved toward us were townsfolk; our relations with ranchers and farmers were not similarly disrupted. But my distance even from ranchers I had known a long time grew more than I realized. For instance, in the summer of 1971 I took two graduate students with me to Short Grass. Working on certain aspects of White social organization, they became friendly with a rancher I had known since my first week in the community and with whose family I had shared many meals. One of my assistants reported that the man's wife had remarked to him: "You gotta watch what you say about Indians around Niels; he gets upset if he thinks you're being too critical."

Methods

Given an interactionist perspective, the participant observation technique seemed most appropriate to this task. Berreman (1962: 24) has noted part of the rationale for this: "Impression management is a feature of all social interaction. . . . Methodological procedures must be employed which will reveal not only the performance staged for the observer, but the nature of the efforts which go into producing it." As a participant, then, the fieldworker must be able to read the communications of his "subjects" and to know what is appropriate behavior. This obviously entails assessing the participants' definitions of social situations and recognizing the images of selves contained in these definitions. The observer must be sensitive to the ways these self-images are projected for each of the participants, not only for himself, and must make careful note of these occurrences. His success in both enterprises depends on the extent to which others interact with him more as a member of the community than as an outsider.[2]

To be sure, this kind of acceptance is an ideal, probably never achieved. It is more likely that the observer will simply achieve a position of trust in the community such that its members do not identify him as one from whom ordinary daily events must be hidden. This involves an increasing admission to "back regions," in Goffman's terms (1959: 238), although the ethnographer—and sometimes even bona fide members of the community—can rarely discover all the information concealed in these secret places. In

[2] To a certain extent, the fact that one never becomes fully a member of the community means not only that certain kinds of information are withheld by one's informants, but also that certain kinds of information are offered. Because the ethnographer has nothing to gain from knowing certain kinds of secrets, he is sometimes entrusted with them (Berreman, 1962: 19) and accorded the role of confidant.

my own fieldwork the problem was to gain access to behavior settings in which Short Grass Indians would communicate things about themselves that were not ordinarily accessible to Whites. I had to be defined as a "safe" person, one who could be trusted not to shatter the delicate balance of Indian-White relationships, and before whom the usual presentation of Indian self-image to Whites could be dropped.

In retrospect, a number of circumstances facilitated this process. One important factor was that of successfully uncarthing and allaying the various suspicions initially provoked by our presence in Short Grass.[3] For example, the immediate suspicion that I was a spy from the Indian Affairs Branch was dispelled when it became clear that I was not a Canadian citizen. It helped that the first car we used belonged to our state university, and that conspicuously stenciled on its sides were the state seal and "For Official Use Only." Over time, the possibility of any connection between myself and the government appeared increasingly remote: IAB agents were conspicuously unenthusiastic about my presence on the reserve, and I had little more success than the Indians themselves at securing material assistance for the band.[4] When it became apparent that my car was as liable to be stopped and searched by Mounties as were those of Indians, the possibility that I was an agent of this arm of the government was similarly discounted. Other, more implausible suspicions also dissipated after the first few months of our stay: that I was a spy for American oil companies; that I was a Communist spy; that I was one of the White men who sometimes entered the reserve in search of the sexual favors of its women; that I was an American draft dodger.

All of this is not to suggest that my wife or I ever became identified as "Indian" (although I did become the adopted son of one

---

[3] See West (1945: ix–x) and Berreman (1962: 8–10) for discussions of these inevitable difficulties.

[4] I made several trips to distant cities, attempting to contact and interview IAB officials, with no success. And I never gained access to any official files regarding the band (there were none kept on the reserve). Consequently, my only contacts with IAB agents occurred when they came to Short Grass, although I was then able to talk with them privately.

couple, and sibling to their children).[5] Instead, since we could not
be placed in any of the White roles familiar to Indians, we were
given a special place in the community. As it became obvious that
we were not government agents or identifiable members of the
local White social structure, and as more immediate personal relationships developed between ourselves and individual Indians,
the apparent self-consciousness of Indians in our company was reduced. On the reserve, Indians did not maintain before me the
usual stoic taciturnity displayed to Whites.

In contrast to the local Whites, we displayed an acceptance of
Indian ways. We did not criticize Indians for their lack of industry
or punctuality, nor did we deliver sermons on the virtues of so-
briety or reliability. We did not show the pervasive White apprehensiveness for the safety of our persons and property, and nothing
of ours was ever locked up. When it became evident that patterns
of everyday Indian behavior normally condemned by Whites did
not arouse our disapprobation, or even our curiosity, measures to
conceal these activities were not taken.

A number of apparent steps in what may be called an "acceptance cycle" indicated the reserve's increasing tolerance, and even
welcoming, of our presence. For example, during my first summer
in Short Grass I had had insurmountable difficulties in talking
with women. If there were no men home when I visited an Indian
house, women would not answer my knocks at the door and pretended there was no one there. In mixed company, women hardly
ever contributed to the conversation, and would avoid even eye
contact on streets in town.[6] During my second visit, and probably
in part because of the presence of my wife, this began to change,
and the women began to act more relaxed in my presence. By the
end of our stay, most of the discomfort seemed to have melted
away: it was not uncommon for me to have tea at an Indian home
with the wife (and other women) when no Indian men were present.

[5] Nothing came of a suggestion, made several times by Indians to a horrified
agent, that our names be officially entered on the band list.
[6] I should mention that at this time women were not permitted in the pubs
in Short Grass, so I had no opportunity to talk with them here. This was
changed several years later in a town election.

Another barometer of our increased acceptance had to do with our participation in religious events. The Sun Dance, for example, involves months of preparation, including four "sings" spaced a couple of months apart, all culminating in the ceremony proper in early summer. When we arrived in the fall of 1966, we were aware that one of these sings was to take place soon, but we did not attend; we had not been invited and did not wish to "intrude." Later we were asked by an Indian friend why we had not shown up. "Everybody expected you'd be there," he said.

We did attend the next sing, a couple of months later. I could not be sure, but it seemed to me that people were generally self-conscious, and that the singing was not particularly enthusiastic (women did not join in at all). My wife and I sat quietly in a corner during the ceremony, which seemed to me rather brief. The singing lasted only a couple of hours before it was broken off for a communal "feast" of sandwiches, corn, tea, and cake. Later, in conversation with an Indian man who had also been present, my suspicions were confirmed: all the Indians there had felt some discomfort and shyness at having Whites present.

By the spring all this had changed, and our attendance at the final sing was quite different from earlier visits. I was directed to sit with the men, my wife moving to the women's side of the room. We participated in the singing, and I was taught how to drum. At intervals, following prayers, I was included in the group of men among whom a stone medicine pipe was circulated. The singing was animated, including both men and women, and it lasted most of the night. We were getting somewhere.[7]

Finally, I think our changing relations with Indian children also indicated a growing ease in our presence. Initially, they were practically invisible, but by the end of the fieldwork they were constantly underfoot with endless small requests: to be given a

[7] One event of the evening took me some time to understand and place in context. We were using a deerskin-covered drum that went slack after a period of pounding; and periodically we had to take it outside and hold it over a fire to tighten the skin. I was thinking how nice it was, to be included in all this when an Indian man said to me: "I wish we had the money to buy one of them regular drums with the screws on the side to tighten, so we wouldn't have to go through this." I thought, but did not say, "But you can't do that, it wouldn't be Indian!"

ride to the beaver dam to swim, to have soda pop brought from
town, to go hunting or sledding, and so on.

Theories

A persistent thread theme in the work of symbolic interactionists is the idea that people are not passive, automatic responders
to external—or even internal—stimuli.[8] True enough, men do
come to inhabit an environment of symbols, which are external and
must be learned in the course of interaction with other human
beings. But the individual is nevertheless an active agent, selec-
tively perceiving and producing symbolic acts. That is, having perceived the symbolic communication of another, he interprets its
meaning, inferring the intent of the other, and responds to this
interpretation. A symbol in this sense is a prelude representing
all that is to follow on the part of the actors. As for the relationship between individuals or groups—i.e. "acting units"—and abstract social structures, Herbert Blumer has unequivocally stated
this position (1962: 189–90):

From the standpoint of symbolic interaction, social organization is a
framework inside of which acting units develop their actions. Structural
features, such as "culture," "social systems," "social stratification," or
"social roles," set conditions for their action but do not determine their
action.... Social organization enters into action only to the extent to
which it shapes situations in which people act, and to the extent to which
it supplies fixed sets of symbols which people use in interpreting their
situations.

A central concept in symbolic interactionism is that of the self.
G. H. Mead (1934: 175) viewed the self as composed of two in-

---

[8] Surprisingly, symbolic interactionism has only recently found a tentative
acceptance among American anthropologists. Given the fact that both anthropology and symbolic interactionism are much concerned with culture as a symbolic system and with the ways it is implicated in day-to-day behavior, a much
earlier rapprochement might have been expected. A few recent studies have
employed the reference-group concept in discussions of acculturation: Hughes
(1957) and Parker (1964) on the Eskimo, French (1961) on the Wasco-Wishram,
and Berreman on the Aleut (1964). Murphy has described symbolic social distance between selves in the practice of male veiling among the Tuareg (1964),
and Berreman has enumerated some of the problems of "impression management" during fieldwork in India (1962). Barth (1966) has attempted to fashion
a "transactional" model of social organization.

separable phases, the I and the Me. "The 'I' is the response of the organism to the attitudes of the others; the 'me' is the organized set of attitudes of others which one himself assumes. The attitudes of the others constitute the organized 'me,' and then one reacts toward that as an 'I.'" Taken together, the I and the Me constitute personality, the I contributing a spontaneous, initiating, and unpredictable quality. Acts are initiated by the I and are given direction, in terms of the expectations of others, by the Me.

There are three consequences of this conception (Meltzer, 1967: 12). First, the individual is "society in miniature," in the sense that he can interact with himself, be ashamed or proud of himself, and so on. Second, since this interaction need not take visible expression, he has a "mind"; self-dialogue occurs. Finally, the individual can, at least potentially, exercise a measure of control over himself and his actions.[9]

One outgrowth of Mead's thought—part of what Kuhn calls "self theory" (1964: 71)—is the dramaturgical perspective, which I shall use here.[10] In this, the individual is seen as performing a part or role, frequently as one of a "team," in circumscribed space and time before an audience (Goffman, 1959: 77–105). During their routines, the actors work both with teammates and with an audience in conveying and receiving communications, which are implicated in the "images of self" associated with the various participants. Bringing off a successful performance involves staging, the management of props and personal appearances, protecting boundaries (as between frontstage and backstage), and in general effectively mastering the art of "impression management." The importance of this last skill lies in the necessity for participants' ex-

[9] This is another point on which anthropologists—or, rather, those anthropologists who reject cultural determinism—and symbolic interactionists would find themselves in substantial agreement. Some anthropologists who have reached this conclusion, each via a somewhat different route, are Opler (1964), Leach (1965: 159–172), and Lee (1959: 5–14).

[10] I use the term perspective rather than theory, since there is as yet no generally accepted body of integrated, formalized propositions for symbolic interactionism. Attempts have been made in this direction, however; see Rose (1962) and Kinch (1963). A kind of dramaturgical perspective has only recently been adopted in anthropology; see, for example, Douglas (1966: 114–28), Turner (1968: 89–127), and the collection of articles on social relations edited by Gluckman (1962).

erting a degree of control over what is communicated about themselves, since information that conflicts with one's intended self-image should not be allowed to slip by.[11] When such mishaps do occur, the actors generally attempt to supply corrective measures and restore integrity to the performance.

The metaphor likening social interaction to drama is really nothing more than that—a metaphor. In real life there is usually serious work to be done, important business to attend to. But the face-to-face symbolic interchange that takes place in mundane contexts is not merely incidental, and the information "games" that accompany human activity are not mere amusements (see Lyman and Scott, 1970: 29–69). The successful completion of a task demands that the flow of information about the task and the participants be effectively maintained. Like a play, this pointed interaction is always bounded in space and limited in time. My own point of reference, for both analysis and observation, will be what Goffman calls "situated activity systems" (1961: 95–99) and the kinds of situated selves that emerge in these circumscribed activities (Goffmann, 1961: 132–43; McCall and Simmons, 1966: 89–94). The performances of interacting individuals will be examined, and the communicative expressions of the actors will be analyzed as claims about their attributes as social beings.

A correctly staged and performed scene leads the audience to impute a self to a performed character, but this imputation—this self—is a product of a scene that comes off, and is not a cause of it. The self, then, as a performed character, is . . . a dramatic effect arising diffusely from a scene that is presented. (Goffman, 1959: 252–53)

In other words, a self is the outcome of communication in social interaction—communication that expressively and impressively conveys information about the actors' social and personal qualities, making it possible for persons to direct their own actions in accordance with their anticipations of one another's behavior.

[11] Indeed, one definition of the self explicitly includes these controlling responses: "The self is any validated program which exercises a regulatory function over other responses of the same organism, including the formulation of other programs" (Stone, 1962: 104).

Another property of human interaction is what has been labeled definition of the situation.[12] Each actor in a situation endeavors to reach an agreement with others regarding which activities are relevant and proper, which are not, and which expressed selves are appropriate to each activity. By expressing himself in a particular way, the actor can attempt to control the others' response to him, thus influencing a definition of the situation that he considers favorable to himself. Ideally, the participants' projections soon adjust to one another, and this "working consensus" forms the context of subsequent transactions. The extent to which the consensus definition is shared in practice, of course, is problematic. What results is usually not

the kind of consensus that arises when each individual present candidly expresses what he really feels and honestly agrees with the expressed feeling of the others present. This kind of harmony is an optimistic ideal and in any case not necessary for the smooth working of society. . . . Together the participants contribute to a single overall definition of the situation which involves not so much a real agreement as to what exists but rather a real agreement as to whose claims concerning what issues will be temporarily honored. (Goffman, 1959: 9 10)

Failure is a crucial possibility, both for definitions of situations and for the situated selves. Selves are sometimes rejected by their putative owners, as happens when a customer in a store mistakenly identifies another customer as a salesman. Intentional claims regarding the possession of a particular self can be deflated by others, as when a bartender refuses to serve a customer he suspects is under age. Or selves can be invalidated when discrepant information comes into the hands of the others present at any point during the interaction. The failures may occur in a number of different ways —intentionally or not, consciously or not, and on the part of any of the participants. In any event, since self-indications and validations by individuals work to define the situation, the situation itself does not come off as intended when they falter. The scene of

[12] This term, coined by W. I. Thomas (1923: 42–44), has become securely entrenched in the behavioral-science vocabulary. See McCall and Simmons (1966) and McHugh (1968) for recent discussions of the concept.

interaction then comes to a halt, either permanently or until some new definition of the situation can be agreed on by the participants (see Strauss, 1959: 35).

Implied in all of this is the presence of a moral dimension to human interaction. In anthropology, the moral imperatives underlying social relationships have long been a subject of special study.[13] In every known society there are omnipresent ideas of right and wrong, of what is proper or improper; and judgments of people's behavior are made according to these conventional standards. The same is true of the definitions governing situations and social selves (Banton, 1965: 57–64). When a person presents evidence bearing on an image of self, the communication has a reciprocally promissory character. As Simmel says (1950: 313), "We base our gravest decisions on a complex system of conditions, most of which presuppose that we will not be betrayed." Individuals, then, are expected not to misrepresent themselves, not to make false claims for secret personal advantage. Of course, such deception nevertheless occurs, often with some regularity.

One factor complicating this view of interaction and the self is the problem of what can be called "multiplicity of selves" (Erikson, 1956). If we focus our attention on the status positions that people occupy in activities with others, and on the roles associated with these positions, we see that a self peculiar to each situation is usually specified for each member of the activity system. As an individual takes his place, his concern is with expressing and maintaining an image of himself as a full-fledged and competent participant who keeps his obligations and expects his due. But these images, and the roles they express, can be quite specialized from situation to situation. Moreover, it is frequently considered improper to permit one of these selves to surface in situations in which it is not ordinarily implicated (Banton, 1965: 151–71). For example, the fact that a preacher is also a lover, a member of a political party, and an athlete is officially irrelevant to his performance in the pulpit, and he is expected not to identify himself

[13] See Redfield (1953: 20–23), Firth (1956: 183–214), and Bidney (1953: 400–432), for some general discussions of this issue.

as any one of these while conducting his services. As Shibutani observes (1962: 139), "Even if one's behavior is inconsistent, as in the case of the proverbial terror of the office who is meek before his wife, it is not noticed if the transactions occur in dissociated contexts." In sum, people are required to compartmentalize or segregate many of their various selves, to restrict what they communicate about themselves to what is situationally relevant.[14] And we must not forget that certain attributes, such as age or sex, may be relevant to a person's performances in many different kinds of situations, whereas other selves may be more narrowly defined.

A related problem arises. If we take one individual as a point of reference, he seems to be something more than a jumble of loosely articulated and occasionally activated selves. There is a subjectively experienced "real" self, which he carries into many situations and which, presumably, lends his existence a sort of continuity.[15] In other words, our "actor" may see himself not as a Machiavellian, calculating player of diverse and contradictory roles, but as a person of some integrity who is, in all of his social intercourse, somehow the same person.

I shall not attempt to present here a definitive solution to these discrepancies. It can be suggested, however, that the way one considers "self" is partly a consequence of perspective. In focusing on situational interaction it is not necessary to assume a kind of consistent, total self for each of the participants, since we are more concerned with the structure and definition of situations, and with the kinds of selves that emerge in them for participants. But if one is concerned with specific individuals as persons, a more biographical approach is appropriate, that is, one that examines the relationships between performed and experienced self-attributes.

The difference is between personal and social identity (Goffman,

[14] See Banton (1965: 167–70) and Turner (1962: 24–26) for discussion of role conflict in this connection.

[15] There are a number of critical discussions of this and allied problems. Deutsch and Krauss (1965: 210–11) have suggested that symbolic interactionism underemphasizes the striving for consistency between the "performed" and the "phenomenal" (felt) selves. Messinger et al. (1962) have treated this problem as a confusion, to some extent, between the ways an observer-analyst treats the self and the way a performer experiences it.

1963b: 51–66, 105–6). An individual's personal identity incorpo-
rates all the things about him, including his name, that in total
give him a biographical uniqueness and set him apart from others.
To understand him personally, one must piece together past and
current events with the various selves he enacts. For example, it
is necessary to ask how he manages to be a figure of authority in
one context and, say, vulnerably dependent in another. In dis-
cussing social identity, by contrast, attention is diverted from dis-
crete persons to the self as a social object, a set of situational attributes that may be assumed by many different individuals.

Of course, it is also possible to investigate the relationship between personal and social identity—to ask, for example, how wide
a latitude is permissible in one's personal "style" of presenting a
social self. Or one can investigate the interactional consequences
of revealed discrepancies between social and personal identities,
as when a man discovers that a trusted business associate once
spent a term in prison for embezzlement.

Finally, from a different perspective, we can concern ourselves
with the individual's "ego identity"—with how he feels about his
personal and social selves, and how these feelings modify his performances. We can ask how mental patients, thrust into a humil-
iating circumstance, respond to identification as sick persons, and
how this response influences their adaptation to institutional life.
Or we may examine the problem of self-esteem, investigating the
conditions under which persons feel their integrity or moral worth
threatened and observing how they deal with this.

In this study I shall work with all three senses of the self: I shall
discuss Indians and Whites as members of social categories with
certain characteristic selves; I shall use examples to illustrate the
way specific persons express these selves in numerous situations;
and I shall examine how persons, especially Indians, respond to
the selves imputed to them in terms of their own perceptions and
feelings about these selves. Two types of interaction will be ex-
plored. The first is of the situated type, in which persons gather
to engage in what are often routine, goal-directed activities. These

tasks—a roundup, a party, a religious or ceremonial observance—
are repeated with varying frequency and regularity, and have relatively stable situational definitions. The second type of interaction
takes place, just as routinely, in public places, where persons are
physically in one another's presence but do not actively cooperate
in joint ventures. It appears that these occasions also have a kind
of structure and are governed by a set of tacit rules (Goffman,
1963a: 193–97). By his mere presence on the streets of town, a
Short Grass Indian conveys information about himself through
his dress, his manner, his behavior toward other passersby, and his
apparent self-involvements. This information, available to any observer, is used to make judgments about the self-attributes of the
observed.

Profanation of the Self

My subject, as stated earlier, has to do with the adjustment of
Short Grass Indians to the fact that their moral worth is denied
by Whites. Now I wish to rephrase this problem in more specialized terms. In later chapters, I shall elaborate on what is meant
when we say that a kind of sacredness is attached to a social self.
I shall discuss the various ways the self may become polluted or
polluting, the specific manner in which this happens to Short Grass
Indians, and the consequences of this for them.

In Western societies (and apparently in many non-Western ones
as well) the social self is ordinarily consigned a certain degree of
sacredness. The "sacred," in this sense, is simply a thing command-
ing awe and respect; and it concerns not only supernatural or
religious matters but also earthly things, including the selves that
people present in daily, face-to-face interaction.[16] In expanding
the ideas of Durkheim, Cooley, and Simmel on this subject, Goffman has pointed out some implications of the sacredness of self,
notably the ceremonial deference that actors pay to one another,

---

[16] See Leach's convincing and illuminating treatment of this subject, in which
sacredness and profaneness are treated as aspects of human action rather than
types of action (1965: 12–13).

which places a measure of social distance between them (1956. 1959: 67–70).[17] By acknowledging the multifarious rules of deference, persons demonstrate reverence for one another's sacredness and for the privacy that it entitles them to. When we speak of matters of etiquette, then, we are not talking about "mere gestures." A self infused with sacredness must be protected from contact with the profane (Durkheim, 1957: 40), and it is social distance that supplies this protection.

When persons are not on terms of intimacy or familiarity, whether they are status equals or not, they have available numerous and elaborate interpersonal rituals through which they can express attraction or avoidance. Attraction is expressed by what Goffman calls "presentational deference," symbolic acts indicating that others are or wish to become involved with the recipient. Salutations, invitations, compliments, and small services all have this effect. Avoidance rituals can act either to protect against defiling a person or to protect against being defiled by him. The coexistence of these two kinds of rules imposes many subtle and paradoxical complexities on social interaction:

In suggesting that there are things that must be said and done to a recipient, and things that must not be said and done, it should be plain that there is an inherent opposition and conflict between these two forms of deference. To ask after an individual's health, his family's well-being, or his state of affairs, is to present him with a sign of sympathetic concern; but in a certain way to make this presentation is to invade the individual's personal reserve, as will be made clear if an actor of wrong status asks him these questions, or if a recent event has made such a question painful to answer. (Goffman, 1956: 487)

The degree of sacredness possessed by any person in a given situation with respect to others present depends on a great many factors, all of which enter into the prevailing definitions of the situation. Rank and status, familiarity or formality, and conventional settings and occasions of interaction all influence both the varieties of regard persons extend to one another and the resulting

---

[17] In Simmel's terms, there is an "ideal sphere" lying around every human being (1950: 321). See also Murphy (1964) and Goodenough (1963: 193), whose treatments of social distance resemble that given here.

social distance between them. Whatever the degree of respect actually offered or demanded, respect itself is necessarily a component of every social interaction.

A clue to why this should be so appears when we examine some attributes of social communication and what are called "identity values" (Goffman, 1963b: 128). In our own society, for example, there are recognized sets of ideal attributes that define a fully worthy male or female. The list is long and demanding: the desirable person should display an attractive appearance, unmarred by slovenliness or by any of a wide inventory of physical defects;[18] he should be respectably employed, have a fine character, and be in full control of his body, his passions, and his will; and he must not be a member of any unpopular social, cultural, or racial group.

The ways in which a person may become socially stigmatized are evidently innumerable, involving any number or combination of failings with respect to identity norms. Some failings, of course, are subject to manipulation: a lack of education or refinement, an undesirable socioeconomic origin, or a discrediting event in personal or family history can easily be concealed. But the individual has little control over other attributes of his social identity—such physical blemishes as a missing limb or a facial birthmark, for example. The commonplace "nobody's perfect" takes on broader meaning when we recognize that no one can realize or embody identity norms perfectly and fully, since no one has absolute control of his person in this respect. A problem for "normal" people, those whose personal defects are not glaringly apparent, is to somehow control the information transmitted about themselves so that discrediting information is not communicated to others. The social distance insinuated between persons by virtue of their regard for one another's sacredness facilitates this. In most social intercourse, there is a sort of gentleman's agreement not to penetrate hidden regions of the self, not to call attention to personal matters that would, if revealed, jeopardize the completion of the activities being undertaken.

[18] See Zetterberg (1966) for a discussion of how people secretly rank one another according to physical and erotic attractiveness.

Interaction is thus, paradoxically, both desirable and menacing: it sets the stage for the realization of a projected and perhaps somewhat idealized self, but at the same time it introduces the danger of failure. Cooley has told us (1964: 251): "By recognizing a favorable opinion of yourself ... you in a measure give yourself and your peace of mind into the keeping of another, of whose attitude you can never be certain." And Murphy (1964a: 1259) has argued that the preservation of social distance is a critical necessity in even the most intimate of relationships: "Interaction is threatening by definition, and reserve, here seen as an aspect of distance, serves to provide partial and temporary protection to the self."

The rules of comportment and courtesy that regulate people's knowledge of one another do not, however, assure that everyone is always endowed with a high degree of sacredness. Some conditions call for a widening or narrowing of social distance. For example, certain categories of people, such as young children or the very old, may be accosted at will by others. It is not considered improper for adults to speak to such people, even though they may be strangers. In the case of a child, a stranger may legitimately request some small errand or other service (this is especially true in small rural communities). Children or elderly persons may be asked for their names and ages, as well as for other kinds of information that strangers may not properly request of other adults; and many (though not all) rules of politeness may be informally dropped with them. One characteristic of these "profane" persons is that they are always recognizable as such: that is, information communicating their position in society is immediately available. Moreover, they cannot disguise themselves or communicate any misinformation about their status that would gain them greater ritual value than they already possess. In many societies, a profane person's movement into another, more sacred position is marked by public recognition of this change in a "rite of passage."

It is also possible for a person to relinquish some of his sacredness when he temporarily enters a role or certain social position that is defined as "open." One is free, for example, to approach salespersons with requests for appropriate services. Or simply being in a certain place can open one's "circle of the self," so that strangers can initiate some interaction; bars, resorts, and cruise ships offer such a setting. Similarly occasions defined as informal may open people to one another. At parties, carnivals, or conventions, reserve is relaxed, social distance is narrowed, and people are free to dispense with the rituals that otherwise separate them. In all these situations, the individual by his very presence commits himself to a definition of the situation that reduces the amount of reverence owed him by others. There is rarely any strongly felt danger of pollution in such social intercourse, since only "unserious" selves are involved. There are other occasions in which a dramatic profanation of self is at issue, in which some of the participants are the subjects of degradation. Anthropology offers many illustrations of this. Gregory Bateson (1958), for example, has described in great detail a degradation ceremony of the New Guinea Iatmul. On various occasions—at adolescent initiation, in ceremonial houses, between men and women in Naven ceremonies —some persons are ritually treated by others in an obscene manner, becoming for the occasion polluted and polluting individuals. Norbeck (1963) has reviewed numerous African "rituals of conflict." In many sub-Saharan societies, on designated ceremonial occasions, "hostility" is symbolically expressed between various categories of persons: men and women, superiors and inferiors, different kin groupings, and formally opposed social and political groups. Among the most spectacular of these ceremonies were the "rituals of rebellion" directed toward Zulu kings, in which commoners could insult and debase royalty.

There have been various interpretations of these debasement rites (e.g., Braroe, 1968), but the symbolic, situational consequences of such a practice are obvious: the recipient of abuse (the king) is temporarily defined as a vile and profane person, whose dignity may be assaulted with impunity. The designation of somebody or something (sometimes even the celebrants themselves) as profane and estranged from the moral order is so pervasive in ritual behavior that perhaps what Turner (1962: 156) observes for the Ndembu is culturally universal: "Among Ndembu it may broadly be said that each major kind of ritual gives plenary or ideal expression to one constituent, or a few closely linked constituents, and excludes, or even expels, whatever is felt to possess a different essence. Thus the concept of pollution may have a situational character for the Ndembu."

In all of the examples I have presented, the socially enacted selves possess sacredness in varying degrees by virtue of their situational circumstance. One is ritually sanctified or defiled by a status position occupied, by a role taken, or by participation in some solemn ceremonial event. The profanation, or sanctification, is often only temporary: children grow up and are assigned greater ritual value; conventioneers return to work and reassume interactional reserve and dignity before their subordinates; a Zulu king is most of the time an exceedingly sacred being. In general, a person's ceremonial value can vary considerably as he participates in a broad range of situations.

On occasion, however, certain recognizable persons become so extremely hallowed or contaminating that their presence is perilous to others in almost every situation they enter. Such was the case with the ancient Hawaiian kings, so invested with *mana* that stringent taboos put them beyond the pale of daily life. At the other extreme are lepers, low-caste untouchables, and other dangerous persons who must be avoided. In these cases, whole categories of persons, and not merely the occupants of a given status, are sacred or profane, carrying the emblems of their ritual value into virtually every situation. One way in which a category of persons can acquire a fixed ritual value is associated with the observance of interpersonal ceremonies. We have noted that everyday interaction involves certain rules of etiquette and propriety, which regulate the degree of social distance between persons. When these rules are persistently violated by a person or group of persons, a permanent loss of sacredness may be entailed.

Trouble-makers who breach the communication line and systematically break the gentleman's agreement concerning communication often pay a price for their liberties. They come to be seen as profane persons, as persons who have sacrificed for gain the respect that is owed them. Once an individual has made this sacrifice, there is little reason why others cannot approach him, since, except for the fact that he may be contaminating, he has no way to hold people off. (Goffman, 1963a: 143–44)

To Short Grass Whites, Indians are such persons.

THREE   The Present

THE TOWN of Short Grass is the social and economic focus of a thinly populated region in the southwestern Canadian Plains. The surrounding 5,000 square miles are inhabited by about 7,400 persons, a third of whom live in the town itself. The Indian reserve is located about 20 miles southeast of town, on what is called the "bench" in the Short Grass hills, which extend for about 60 miles east to west, and rise to 4,000 feet, some 1,400 feet above the elevation of the town itself. Ranching and various types of farming are the economic bases of the rural population throughout the district, and thus the indirect support of most Short Grass townspeople. The average ranch is five times the size of the average farm (10 sections versus 2, or 6,400 acres versus 1,280 acres), and farms outnumber ranches about 10 to 1. Most of the 90-odd ranches are located in the hills or on their slopes.

The weather, both severe and unpredictable, is a major concern of all residents of the region. One Short Grass rancher wrote me in the fall of 1969: "We have had a bad year out here in the hills. The hay crop froze on the 11th of June, when it was nice and green. ... I never made a bale this year." Such events can bring disaster, and bounty years are often followed by lean ones. Although the growing season is short, ranches and farms can be operated profitably if the right amount of moisture is available. But the uncertainty of conditions introduces a great element of risk into these enterprises (Bennett, 1963). Winter, for example, may bring spectacular blizzards that destroy property and cattle, followed by rapid thaws—and floods—when a warm "chinook" blows up from the Rocky Mountains. In the spring, freezes, drought, or hailstorms can wipe out a year's crop.

The population of the region has fluctuated historically along with climatic changes. In the 1930's and 1940's there was an exodus of homesteaders who could not cope with those years of drought and depression. Similarly, many of the hamlets and villages that had been established in the area during the first two decades of the century either declined or simply vanished. The population of Short Grass itself, however, is steadily increasing, since it has become the service center for the entire region and is also a favored place of retirement for ranchers and farmers.

There is some variation in the style and scale of ranching in the region. Ranchers on the elevated "bench" land are mostly the descendants of the earliest pioneers, and operate small, relatively marginal enterprises. As a group they also have the greatest social intercourse with Indians. At the other extreme are the "town ranchers," who occupy larger holdings on the northern slope of the hills and are generally more affluent and more active in town affairs. In terms of occupational prestige, and in the extent to which they influence local society and culture, all the Short Grass ranchers have an importance out of proportion to their numbers. A sign on the outskirts of town introduces Short Grass as "the Old Cow Town," and this image is taken seriously. The prevailing mode of dress is Western, and the most conspicuous community events are the yearly stampedes, or rodeos. A number of roping and saddle clubs seek to perpetuate the skills of the cowboy; and the town newspaper regularly publishes the reminiscences of local "old-timers," who have formed a prestigious club that maintains a small museum of pioneer relics and memorabilia. When a hundred or so old daguerreotype plates were discovered in the basement of an old building not long ago, copies were made and widely circulated, and there was considerable conjecture and discussion about the people and places pictured.

The desirable attributes of the ideal man in Short Grass fit the familiar Western mystique: self-reliance, honesty, a willingness to help others, respect for and ability to cope with nature, friendliness tempered by a desire for privacy, gallantry toward the opposite sex, and independence. Subtle rules of etiquette, sometimes broken by outsiders, reflect the local admiration for these qualities. For instance, one rancher complained about a visitor to the region who had innocently asked him the size of his herd (the number of cattle a man "runs" is a good indication of his annual income): "*I* don't go around asking people how much their salary is, or how much they got in the bank." In Short Grass, conversations between ranchers in a cafe or pub are ordinarily held in guarded terms; one does not tell others exactly what one's calving rate was or how many calves have been lost, nor does one request such information of others.

Farming, both straight grain and mixed, is predominant in the flattest areas of the prairie, north and south of the hills. And the Short Grass region contains several mixed-farming colonies of Hutterites, all established between 1951 and 1960. Hutterites are a German-speaking Anabaptist sect ethnically and ideologically related to the Mennonites and Amish. Economically the most successful of any group in the region, these communal "foreigners" occupy 4 percent of the land and constitute 7 percent of its population. But in spite of their economic significance to the region, social relations between them and other Whites are minimal, and those with Indians nonexistent. Small groups of Hutterites occasionally visit town, but their alien dress and speech signify their removal from ordinary social intercourse.

Short Grass, though the largest town in the region, is nevertheless quite small—about 10 to 12 short blocks square. Until five years ago, all its streets were unpaved, including those of the "business" district. The houses are small and well kept, with diminutive lawns laboriously nurtured on the dry soil. As the service center for a large area, the town does offer a great deal. It has a consolidated school system to which rural children are brought by bus, a modern hospital and clinic, and a dozen churches. There are a livestock auction ring, a town hall, a community hall, and an animal hospital. Businesses include two banks, five cafes, two hotels (both operating public beer halls[1]), three drugstores, a few small shops selling hardware and dry goods, and two large supermarkets, one of which is part of a larger community co-op. Finally, there are a number of farm-equipment dealers, garages, and service stations.

Short Grass is relatively isolated, and except during the hunting season or at stampede times one does not see many strangers on the streets. Very little provincial, national, or international news is reported in the town's weekly paper—although television, now nearly ubiquitous, has given Short Grass residents an increasing knowledge of such matters. There is a small city about 60 miles away, but it is infrequently visited. Short Grass is almost five miles off the major highway leading to the city, and this portion of the highway was completed only 15 years ago. North-south communication is still very poor: the roads to the United States, about a hundred miles away, are unpaved and impassable in winter. Only the few most affluent of the town's Whites can afford extended vacations in the outside world. For most, an excursion to the famous Calgary Stampede or a shopping trip to Great Falls, Montana, is an unusual and long-remembered treat.[2]

---

[1] The provincial liquor regulations are relatively complex (as of 1968). Licensed beverage rooms, which serve only beer and wine, can be housed only in hotels. They open from 11 A.M. to 6:30 P.M., close for dinner, and reopen from 8 P.M. to 11:30 P.M. In Short Grass an election was held five years ago to permit women to drink in the pubs, and both pubs now have a section reserved for "accompanied ladies." Regulations are quite precise. For example, there cannot be more than two full glasses of beer per person at a table, and one may not move one's beer oneself from one table to another—the waiters must do this. Waiters can and do refuse service to anyone they think has had enough, or who uses "foul" or loud language. The pubs also bar troublesome customers for a week or so; an occasional offender may be forbidden service permanently. The state-operated liquor store is open five days a week until 6 P.M. One is permitted to purchase liquor only for one's own use, and it may not be consumed in public places or on the Indian reserve; nor may one have any open bottles in a car. This, of course, presents a knotty problem for Indians, who may now legally purchase whiskey but have no place to drink it legally.

[2] As we shall see, Short Grass Indians are much more mobile than Whites. They visit the "States" several times a year and frequently make impulsive trips to distant reserves and cities, sometimes remaining at these places for several months at a time.

Not all of Short Grass's institutions affect Indians directly, nor is all of its social space open to Indians. In later chapters this will be discussed in detail, but some preliminary observations may be presented here.

Indians are not involved in such White community organizations as churches, saddle clubs, the Chamber of Commerce, the Rotary, or the Old-timers' Association. There are occasional token gestures: one elderly Indian was invited to a banquet of the Old-timers' Association several years ago, during the town's Diamond Jubilee celebration; and the Rotary recently sponsored a Christmas party for Indian children. However, no organized charitable assistance is extended to Indians.[3] And Indians themselves never seek the assistance of local government representatives such as the agricultural officer, the public health nurse, or the veterinarian. These officials, in turn, do not visit the reserve to offer their services. Indians do not make use of the town credit union, the lawyer's office, or the livestock auction. And certain small businesses—beauty salons, the bakery, gift and florist shops, and furniture or jewelry stores—rarely see an Indian customer.

Some places in town are tacitly forbidden to Indians, and they are informed in various ways that their presence is not welcome. For example, the cafes are stratified, and Indians are discouraged from entering those that are frequented by the Short Grass elite. Until recently, one cafe had a sign posted on the door reading "No Indians Allowed." Similarly, there is a provincial park twenty miles from town with extensive recreational facilities—restaurant, swimming pool, small lake, golf course, and riding stable—and to my knowledge no Indian ever visited the place.

[3] An instructive transaction occurred during my residence in 1966–67. A local church group agreed to assist the band in setting up an "Indian Friendship Center" in town where Indians might gather for coffee, so that they would have some place other than the pubs to frequent and would not have to loiter in public places. At a meeting between a group of adult Indian males, an Indian agent, and church representatives, it was suggested by the last group that this facility be set up on the reserve itself, which was unacceptable to the Indians. As some Whites later told me, it was feared that the Indians might use the Center as a place to drink and/or spend the night instead of returning to the reserve. At the time I left, no decision had been reached, and the matter appeared to have been dropped indefinitely.

By contrast, there are places frequented almost exclusively by Indians, such as the "nuisance grounds" (dump) on the edge of town. Until the town council had them demolished about five years ago, there were several small shacks there, built by Indians. Now, in good weather, Indians gather there to spend the night, even pitching tents during stampede time rather than returning to the reserve. In effect, housing is unavailable in town, and Indians are refused rooms in the hotels. I noted two exceptions. One elderly man rented a dilapidated house for several months, but was forced to vacate because of "rowdy parties and trouble with the police," as a local White phrased it. The other exception was the family of the only regularly employed Indian man. After renting a neatly kept house in town for several years, they moved back to their home on the reserve.

The Reserve Community

From Short Grass one reaches the Indian reserve over roads that are unpaved and in some places merely trails across the prairie. Usually the trip is about a half hour's drive; but during the winter the roads are frequently impassable, and melting snow in spring or a heavy summer rain can create a thick, sticky "gumbo" through which travel is possible only on horseback or by tractor.

Although land has been added to the reserve several times, it is still quite small. All Indian families live on the original, one-section tract.[4] With the additional sections adjoining this, there are altogether 3,040 acres of land, much of it unsuitable for farming because of the rocky soil and the dense cover of aspen bush. The reserve has not been partitioned off into individually owned parcels, and aside from the space taken up by homesites, the land is held jointly. Cattle ranching is the only feasible agricultural

[4] The road from town enters the reserve from the north and forks to the northwest and southwest corners of this section. The "lower camp" in the northwest includes five households. The reserve slopes upward from the north to the crest of the Short Grass hills in the south, where the two households of the smaller "upper camp" are located. The remaining households are strung along the winding road that connects the two camps, and the boarded-up schoolhouse is about midway along this.

activity, since even the short growing season at this altitude allows
a moderate yield of winter fodder from the flat bench land of the
reserve. But even if the reserve land were exploited to its maxi-
mum capacity, it would only provide a marginal existence for one
small family (as we have seen, the average ranch in the district is
more than twice this size). Several Indian families do keep small
herds of cattle, but these do not and could not provide all their
needed income. Given such limited resources, the entire reserve
community cannot maintain itself by either ranching or farming.

The ease with which Indians come and go makes it difficult to
give precise population figures for the reserve. There are always
a few visitors from other reserves living temporarily in various
households, and at any given time, a few members of the Short
Grass band will be visiting or working away from the reserve. A
census in 1963 showed that of a hundred-odd residents men were
slightly outnumbered by women, and that about half the reserve
population was under 16 years old. The preponderance of women
and children is undoubtedly due to a reduced mortality rate
among mothers and infants, a result of the improved medical care
in recent years and of the fact that most Indian women have their
babies at the community hospital in Short Grass. A few people
have actually migrated to other reserves, changing their band
membership, and a few have similarly moved to the reserve to
live with their spouses. To my knowledge, however, no Short Grass
Indian has migrated to any city. During my fieldwork, about 15
other Indians who were not band members were also living more
or less permanently on the reserve, including one family of "outsiders" who were not on the band list of any reserve.

During the period of this study, there were 11 households on
the Short Grass reserve, ranging in size from 5 to 15 members. Four
of these households included only a nuclear family (a man and
his wife and children). One other nuclear family had been away for
several years, living near other reserves and occasionally returning
to Short Grass for brief periods. Five households included members from three generations, and one had four generations repre-

sented. Household composition, however, is constantly shifting, and during my stay there were several changes: an aged widow, occupying a small house alone, who died; an unmarried woman with three small children who first lived in a separate household and later moved in with her father; a "bachelor" living alone, whose wife had deserted him and who later left his house unoccupied when he went to work on a distant ranch; and two brothers who were living together, with their wives and children, while a house for one of them was being built.

The explanation for this instability in household constitution lies partly in Indian marriage practices. With the exception of one couple, none of the marriages on the reserve are legal by Canadian law. There is no formal ceremony (there was not aboriginally); and marriage is the exclusive concern of the man and woman involved. By White standards parents are permissive regarding the sexual alliances of their adolescent children, and there is no social stigma attached to "illegitimacy," though female promiscuity meets with disapproval. Young Indians, especially girls, subscribe to the notions of romantic love; and, following a brief courtship, it is usual for a couple to simply take up residence together, most often at the girl's home.[5] Should the "marriage" fail—the most usual causes are jealousy, quarreling over money, or the abuse of one partner by the other—it is dissolved, and husband or wife returns home. Any children usually remain with the mother. I encountered nine single Indians with children, including two men who were estranged from their wives and living with their parents and one older woman whose husband had committed suicide some eight years previously.

A marriage is regarded as stable by the reserve community only after man and wife have lived together for about a decade, have had children, and have gradually adjusted to each other. There

[5] Whether or not some form of cultural continuity is involved, it is of interest that aboriginally a Cree husband owed "bride service" to his wife's family. The couple would spend the first several years residing with them, and the groom was expected to contribute his labor and hunting skills to their support (Mandelbaum, 1940: 245).

were 10 such unions during my longest stay, each one the basis of a household.[6] Three newlywed couples, one childless, also lived on the reserve at the time I left in 1967. This number had varied as alliances changed and as young people returned from other reserves with new husbands or wives. The reverse was also true: several young Short Grass Indians, of both sexes, were living with new spouses on distant reserves.

Young Cree, it should be apparent, are remarkably mobile both as individuals and as couples. They habitually visit other communities, sometimes for quite lengthy stays, to attend dances, to work, or simply for a change of scenery. At these times small children and infants are customarily left with their grandparents, to be indulgently cared for; and in some cases the grandparents seem to have permanently taken over the rearing of the children. Charlie and Mary Antelope, for example, had up to 15 children living with them at various times. This is not a new phenomenon, and many of the older Indians on the reserve were themselves raised by their own grandparents.

From adults, whether relatives or not, Cree children almost always receive demonstrative affection and permissiveness. They are never corporally punished (see Pettitt, 1946); they are free to play, eat, and sleep as they please; and they are included in nearly all adult activities. At one winter religious observance I attended, dozens of children of all ages were noisily moving around in a crowded house as the adults present participated in the ceremony; no attempts were made to quiet or restrain them.

In the mid-1960's all the reserve dwellings were boxlike plywood cabins measuring about 20 by 25 feet. Most had one or two small bedrooms (without doors) partitioned off from a combination kitchen and living room. In all but two houses the interior walls were painted, and the flooring throughout was invariably pro-

[6] Government policy is influential in this regard. One IAB agent claimed to respect what he called "blanket marriage" but refused to build a house for a young, recently wed couple with one child. He told the husband he would consider doing so only if they became legally married, and later commented to me: "Why should I give them a $3,000 house when they'll probably bust up in six months anyway?" This is, of course, another source of marital instability.

vided by several layers of worn linoleum. There was neither running water nor electricity on the reserve, and heat was supplied by old-fashioned, wood-burning kitchen stoves. Neither were there barns or other specialized outbuildings, although several households used nearby abandoned log cabins as storehouses and animal shelters.

Houschold furnishings were sparse. Each house had been built with a set of kitchen cabinets and an unusable sink. In the main room, there would be a dining table with chairs or benches, a washstand, and sometimes an old dresser. There were at the most three beds, and those who could not be accommodated in these, usually children, slept on the floor. Two houses had sofas (the only overstuffed furniture on the reserve), and two women owned treadle sewing machines. Each household had a small complement of cooking and eating utensils, and few other housekeeping implements aside from a broom, a mop, flatirons that were heated on the stove, and so on. Most Indian women complained that it was very difficult to keep their places clean because of soot from the stoves and the lack of running water. No house had curtains or window shades, and the only decorations were occasional calendars or pictures torn from a magazine.

It is extremely difficult to specify the annual income of any given household, and nearly impossible to do so for the reserve as a whole. Indians are reluctant to report their earnings, since this could jeopardize their receiving full relief payments. Moreover, many common sources of income—such as the selling of hay from reserve land or the cutting of fenceposts from a nearby forest preserve—are illegal and therefore go unmentioned. Finally, and most important, Short Grass Indians themselves do not know with any accuracy what their incomes are, since they keep no records of income or expenditure. It is possible, however, to indicate the various sources of income and their relative importance.

Every reserve family receives a monthly relief payment, administered through the Indian Affairs Branch. Each head of household must reapply for this each month, listing all household members and all other sources of income. In the mid-1960's, the largest household, which included two adults and 15 dependent children and grandchildren, received $160.00 per month; the smallest monthly payment was $37.00, to a young couple with one child.

To supplement the scanty relief payments, virtually all reserve households engage in the manufacture and sale of fenceposts. This is a cooperative venture. Poplar trees are cut in the bush by both men and women and are hauled in by horsedrawn wagon. In a cleared area near the house the posts are sawed to the proper length, sharpened by axe, and soaked in a barrel of copper sulfate preservative ("bluestone") for three or four hours. A family can easily produce 100 posts a day, or 150 with a little extra effort. Whether these are sold to the lumberyard in town or directly to ranchers, the going rate is 10 to 20 cents per post, depending on the quality of manufacture and the current demand. Theoretically, even a small family could earn some $300 a month in this way, but in practice posts are generally cut only when money is required for some specific purpose: to pay a fine, to travel to a stampede, or to meet the expenses of the Sun Dance. No family works steadily at cutting posts. Occasionally, Indians will contract with a rancher to cut posts for him from his own land, but this never involves more than several days' work.

Working for White ranchers and farmers is another source of income, though an unpredictable one for most of the year. Usually, a rancher will ask a particular Indian to help with a job such as spring branding or repairing fences; but again, the work seldom lasts for more than a few days. The most active period is late July through early August, when ranchers begin to harvest and stack bales of hay for the winter. At this time, a rancher may hire an Indian off the street in town, or even visit the reserve looking for workers. Payment is usually $10 a day. But Indians often demand to be paid at the end of each day; and since this usually means that they will not show up for the next day's work, most ranchers do not like to hire them on this basis.

The more common arrangement is for an Indian family to set up a tent on the ranch itself and remain there until the job is completed, at which time they are paid by the bale. As an example, in

1967 Harry Deersleep, his two adult sons, their wives and children, and one unrelated adult male camped on a ranch about 30 miles from the reserve. At five cents a bale, with the help of the women and the use of the rancher's trucks, they moved and stacked 16,000 bales in two weeks and were paid $800. This was the eighth year running that the family had worked for the same rancher, and most reserve families have similar arrangements with other Whites. In a variation of this pattern, a group of young Indian men will sometimes travel through the immediate district soliciting contracts to haul hay at a piece rate. One group of five was able to make as much as $120 on a good day. However, they worked sporadically: earnings would be spent immediately on new clothing, trips, and so on; and when the cash on hand ran out they would go out in search of further work.

It is also possible for Indians to secure temporary employment on a number of beet and potato farms that lie about 200 miles west of Short Grass. These are quite extensive operations, and recruiters from the farms visit the reserve each summer to hire men and women for the harvest at hourly wages of $1 for women and $1.25 for men, with living quarters provided. Relatively few Short Grass Indians make use of this opportunity: in the summer of 1966 only one couple and one bachelor worked on the farms, and the couple quit after earning the down payment for a used truck.

This reluctance to take distant wage labor is not due to an unwillingness to be away from home; rather, it reflects the Indians' orientation toward work in general. Hauling bales or cutting posts is something that one can do to raise money quickly for some specific purpose, and when the necessary sum is earned the reason for working evaporates. Living on the potato farms, by contrast, entails daily expenses for food and the like, as well as a certain outlay for sociable pursuits like drinking or gambling. It is possible to return to Short Grass after several months with nothing to show for one's time. An immediate need for one or two hundred dollars can be satisfied much faster by staying near the reserve.

I observed two significant exceptions to the generally irregular mode of employment in the reserve community. One man had

worked and lived for 10 years on two prosperous ranches and had
withdrawn from the reserve community; but in 1966, after a period
of heavy drinking and several arrests, he became "unemployable,"
and returned to the reserve. The second exception was a man who
worked for four years for the provincial highway department. He
was the only reserve member with a regular income and lived in
town, though maintaining his house on the reserve. By the end of
my fieldwork he, too, had quit his job and had returned to live
on the reserve.

By "leasing" of land to Whites, selling hay, and charging "grazing fees" to ranchers, some band members occasionally acquire additional cash—never more than several hundred dollars per year
and ordinarily much less. These financial arrangements are informal, complicated, and ambiguous; and they are a constant source
of friction between Indians and Whites, between ranchers, and
between Indians themselves. According to law, proceeds from the
sale of communally owned resources on the reserve are supposed
to be deposited in a government-supervised "band fund," which
is intended to provide for reserve maintenance and improvement.
But numerous clandestine deals are made between individual Indians and Whites, and as a result the band fund never contains
more than a hundred dollars.

There are other, very minor sources of income—a small child
allowance paid to all Canadian parents, old-age pensions collected
by two men on the reserve, and similar miscellaneous items. For
example, at the yearly stampede Short Grass Indians are customarily paid a small sum to organize and stage a wagon race for
spectators.

Small-scale ranchers and farmers in the Short Grass region, after
paying production costs, average around $2,000 income yearly
(Bennett, 1969: 100). As nearly as it is possible to determine, the
income of most Indian families is not significantly less than this.
Appearances would indicate otherwise: in contrast with White
establishments, Indian households are poorly equipped, and many
Indians seem to be chronically without money for basic necessities
such as food and clothing; even in winter not more than a week's

supply of groceries and staples is kept on hand. The discrepancy can be traced to patterns of consumption, as well as those of employment. From the White point of view, Indians do not use their income wisely, do not exercise "deferred gratification" (see Schneider, 1953). Instead of putting aside money for future needs, they generally spend it at once on "trifles"—liquor, a trip to Montana, an old car or truck, or a court fine. Consequently, they have far less to show in terms of agricultural equipment or household furnishings than do Whites with a comparable income. Moreover, with the exception of the monthly relief payments, Indians receive their money irregularly and unpredictably. Whites receive most of their income in regular wages or from the periodic sale of tangible assets like cattle or crops, and for this reason they can easily obtain credit in Short Grass; but Indians can seldom accumulate sufficient resources at any one time to allow a large capital investment in goods or machinery, and they receive credit only in the form of small personal loans.

The legal status of the Short Grass band is somewhat anomolous, for it is one of the few "nontreaty" Indian groups in western Canada. Substantively, this means that its members do not receive the annual payment of $5 per person provided for by treaties made in the late nineteenth century.[7] More important, however, is the band's ambiguous relationship to the Indian Affairs Branch, which does not seem able to deal efficiently with a nontreaty reserve. Numerous attempts have been made to persuade the Short Grass band to move east to some larger reserve; but the Indians have stubbornly refused, claiming that there is no work to be found there, or that they fear the violence believed to be common on the larger reserves. The IAB has always been reluctant to provide funds for developing the Short Grass reserve, probably because of its small size and isolation. Recently, however, there seems to

---

[7] In 1966 there was some discussion on the reserve about being "put on treaty." Some were enthusiastic, hoping that the band would then receive retroactive payments for the preceding decades. But after the local agent firmly insisted that this would not be possible, the Indians became apprehensive that treaty status might affect their relief payments or result in more supervision by the government, and the subject was dropped.

have been some acceptance of the Indians' determination to remain where they are, and a few efforts have been made to improve reserve conditions.

The last concerted attempt to remove the band came in 1957. The band chief of that time accepted the IAB proposals; but when the rest of the band (including his three married sons) still refused to migrate, he went east alone and changed his band affiliation. This incident apparently impressed the IAB with the Cree's determination, and it then acted to assist the band. The then agent, who retired shortly afterward, is still remembered with fondness by the Indians, who claim that he was the last IAB representative to really care about their welfare.

This was the period when White families were moving off the bench, and the land of one such rancher, with 80 of his cattle, was purchased to enlarge the reserve. The same man contracted with the IAB to build houses to replace the log shacks Indians were then living in, and he completed 10 of the 11 plywood buildings still in use. Some agricultural equipment was provided for the band, including a horse-drawn mower and two hay rakes. A school was constructed with a small attached apartment for the teacher and his family (the only buildings with electricity). A road was graded to connect the two camps on the reserve to the school. Finally, it was at this time that Indians began receiving relief payments.

Following this phase of activity, the reserve community was once again neglected. The Indians allowed the new equipment to rust and did not build fences. Many of the cattle were sold, and others were left to starve, or were eaten. A series of agents who visited the reserve (there has never been a resident agent there) were disappointed: in spite of the government's efforts to help, the Indians did not seem to them willing to cooperate. One agent probably represented the attitude of the IAB, at least unofficially, when he remarked to me in 1963: "This bunch is pretty much a hopeless case. We'll probably have to support them all forever." In the Indians' view, the government remained indifferent toward them for a decade.

In 1967, however, there was a renewal of interest in the band, and several new projects were begun. More roads were graded, and in the summer work crews began installing lines to carry electricity to all the houses on the reserve.[8] During these months, IAB agents paid more visits to the reserve than they had over the preceding three years. Plans were discussed to reopen the school and begin adult education classes for those interested. In spite of past failures with cattle ranching—of the animals distributed in 1957 only two households still had a few left—a new scheme was instituted to encourage this enterprise. Two brothers, Johnny and Gordon Antelope (the latter quitting his job with the highway department at this opportunity), were able to raise a nominal purchase price for 15 head of cattle (the largest share of the cost was paid by the IAB), which the agent bought for them locally. These were all impregnated cows, and the men were to keep the female calves, selling all males except one to be reserved as a service bull; at the end of three years, the original 15 head were to be returned to the IAB. With further assistance, the brothers purchased a used tractor and baler and began putting up winter feed. These two men were the only ones selected to participate in the experiment. Among their age-mates, they had had the fewest scrapes with the police and were judged the most responsible.

The short history of the reserve school is a fairly representative example of the difficulties that the IAB has experienced with the Short Grass band. This was the first exposure of most of the Indian children to formal education,[9] and the results were not promising

---

[8] This work was completed several months after I had left the reserve. Characteristically, all households had raised the money to buy a TV set within a few weeks of the time power was switched on, as I was informed in a letter from an Indian man. By 1971, however, half the households again had no power; it had been switched off by the electric company for nonpayment of bills.

[9] Only one adult male on the reserve—the father of Johnny and Gordon Antelope—is literate in English. In 1911 he and several other young Indians had been rounded up by the Mounted Police and placed in an Indian boarding school, where he remained for eight years. Five adult women who had been raised on other reserves could also read and write English. With one exception, however, all adults over 35 could write Cree, using a system of notation invented in the last century by a Protestant missionary.

It is doubtful if much was even communicated, since none of the
children under six or seven spoke English and none of their succession of teachers spoke Cree. Attendance was extremely poor,
and some parents kept their children more or less permanently
out of school. In class, the pupils were quiet, unresponsive, and,
to the teachers, maddeningly expressionless.

The rewards of teaching on the reserve appear to have been
meager enough to discourage teachers quickly. In the eight years
the school operated there were five teachers, the first four lasting
only a year each. None of them spoke Cree or attempted to learn
the language. A Protestant minister took the job to begin with.
Local ranchers will recount, with great amusement, how the Indians' "morals" brought him close to a nervous breakdown. His
successor also left in disgust, contending that it was impossible to
teach the students—when they were present at all—and impossible
to persuade the parents to behave decently and set an example.
The third teacher came determined to "straighten them out," but
only managed to win the active hatred of the entire reserve community by his patronizing lectures on morality. At least twice, dogs
were set on him. His replacement was a man who had been crip-
pled by polio, and his inability to move about compounded the
problems that all of his predecessors had faced. He did not fare
well with either the Indians or the IAB, and complained that the
government did not provide him with the support necessary to
accomplish his job.

The final teacher, Mr. Sterling, was a man with somewhat more
realistic goals and a greater force of character than the others.
His views were paternalistic and his methods arbitrary, but he
seems to have been genuinely fond of the Indians, young and old.
He had his own views on the "Indian problem":

You can really do too much for people, so that you rob them of their
initiative. Hell, these people are getting paid for *not* working. . . . What
should be done is to give them jobs at the same salaries that Whites
would get and then let them sink or swim. This would cost a lot initially,
but it would pay off in the long run. They'd eventually get the idea and
start to become self-supporting.

Sterling lived nearly four years on the reserve with his wife and five children, taking over many of the duties of an agent. His solution to school attendance was to refuse to forward the monthly relief applications of families whose children were repeatedly absent. He attempted to keep the illegal sale of such reserve resources as hay and cattle to a minimum, and informed the government when he suspected that some irregularity was taking place. He often gave Indians rides to town or to the hospital, and was hopeful that some of his students "would see the inside of the high school—if their parents don't let them quit at sixteen." However, like those before him, he eventually grew disillusioned. Since, in addition, his family was unhappy with the isolated reserve life, he elected to move on. Attempts to educate Indian children on the reserve itself were abandoned, and they are now bussed to school in town. The reserve school was boarded up and has remained so. On several occasions large Indian families requested the use of the former teacher's quarters as a dwelling, but all were refused.

It is too soon to tell whether going to a White school will produce more tangible and, to the government, more satisfactory results. Attendance is still a problem: the bus frequently cannot make it to the reserve in winter, and when it does there are invariably some children left behind. Teachers still complain that their Indian pupils are unresponsive, that they do not play with the White children, and that they do not possess the language skills needed to grasp what is presented to them.

All in all, the reserve's history of relations with the federal government through local IAB agents has been a checkered one, marked by alternate periods of assistance and apparent unconcern. But always visible have been the agents' paternalistic authority and their quickness to express disapproval of their charges and frustration with their own failure to exercise a civilizing influence. The following is characteristic. A new agent, who had briefly visited Short Grass once before, came with an assistant to spend several days. After touring the reserve and contacting influential ranchers and Short Grass town officials, he called a meeting with the band for the afternoon of his second day. His mistake was to have arranged this on the day relief checks arrived. I recorded the events shortly after the meeting:

This afternoon I met [Agent] David Bradford upstairs over the town hall to await the Indians at 2 P.M. We chatted for a half hour, getting acquainted, and he was becoming visibly irritated that nobody had showed up yet. "I *did* tell them two, didn't I?" he said to the other agent. Affirmative. After another twenty minutes, and growing evidence of pique from Bradford, Oscar Lodgeskins and two of his teenage sons saunter in (there is a distinct aroma of wine). They are followed by Helen Antelope, with a couple of small ones in tow. Stragglers appear, including the Antelope brothers, Sam Timber, Bighorn, and some of the Antelope clan. . . . There are perhaps 25 Indians of various ages present, all of the adults in some stage of inebriation (Oscar is asleep and snoring). Bradford seems reluctant to start with so few, and kills time talking with individuals, e.g., with Jimmy Deersleep about getting Margaret a health-insurance card. When it appears that few others are going to show up, he calls the meeting to order. This is at 3:15.

Jimmy asks immediately for the floor and begins a ten-minute speech. Although he gesticulates expressively, the dignity of his oratory is marred by an alcoholic incoherence: he frequently gets lost and pauses to retrieve the train of his argument. Bradford and assistant exchange ill-disguised shrugs and glances of woe. Jimmy ends with something like, "If we're gonna make this place a good place to live, then we got to . . . to . . . get together, an' . . . an' . . . get busy." He drops his upraised palm and says, "That's all I have to say. I am done," and sits down.

Bradford begins, doomed to failure, to present plans for the community, constantly interrupted by "irrelevant" questions—e.g., Louis Scarbelly asks if he can get some money for bus fare for his son, stranded in Battleford. After another half hour, Bradford adjourns the "meeting," visibly angered but tight-lipped. He tells them that he'll call another meeting after he's had a chance to look around some more. As a body, the Indians depart noisily.

I hang around for a few minutes while they gather up their papers, Bradford thrusting them into his briefcase. He eyes the door to see that no one's there, and says to me, "I don't believe it! A whole band drunk! What can you *do* with a bunch like this? Is it like this all the time? And where in the hell was the chief, he promised me he'd be here." I make a noncommittal remark to the effect that the first of the month is always an occasion for a little celebration. Bradford says he has an appointment with Pete Wilcox (a town councillor), and we part.

In Short Grass, anyone purchasing beer "to go" from a pub or liquor from the government store must fill out a slip giving his name and listing the items purchased. That afternoon, I discovered, the agent visited these places to determine the total of the Indians' purchases. In the evening he angrily reported to me the results of his survey: "Do you know they spent over two hundred dollars today on liquor? Imagine! And that doesn't count whatever they spent on beer in the pubs! And the evening isn't over yet!" As a result of his discoveries he determined to put the band on non-cash relief; that is, he would have their checks deposited at one of the general stores, where they could draw food and clothing.[10]

The other government representatives significant in the lives of Indians are the Royal Canadian Mounted Police, who at Short Grass perform some of the functions a resident agent might. About a dozen officers work out of Short Grass (the town has no municipal police as such) and all of these rotate frequently. As a consequence, they do not know the Indians well as individuals. Mounties do not enter the reserve often, and then only on a specific errand –for example, to pick up a tuberculosis patient and escort him to a sanatorium.[11] They will also come to search for an Indian wanted for some offense, such as failing to pay a fine. At such times, their ignorance of the reserve and its inhabitants usually leads to failure, and the "fugitive" either hides in the bush or remains anonymous.

---

[10] As a postscript to this, the following was recorded by my wife. *Bradford visit to reserve, May 23–25:* Bradford came by the house looking for Niels at ten in the morning, after having completed another visit to the reserve. Niels was in Regina. Bradford had a message for him to call Fergusson. Then, before parting, he said he had gone up to the reserve and looked it over, and he had talked to shopkeepers in town to see how the money-grocery arrangements were working. Bradford was disappointed to have found out that the Indians were making cash money by cutting posts. His stratagem of depriving the Indians of cash for liquor had not worked out the way he thought it would.

[11] TB is the most serious health problem on the reserve. About once a year, a doctor and a public-health nurse go to the reserve to give chest X-rays to band members—or at least to those who will consent to the examination. Over the 1963–67 period, approximately 10 percent of the reserve population was hospitalized for durations up to two years because of the disease. Treatment seems to have been effective, inasmuch as there were no deaths caused by TB.

Thursday morning. A group of us, mostly Antelopes, lounged outside
old Charlie's house, chatting and exchanging jokes. Green and another
Mountie appeared, looking for Leonard Antelope, who was to be hospitalized. They pulled up to the house, got out, and asked Delbert if he
knew where Leonard was, to which the reply was negative. Then Green
asked Leonard if he had seen Leonard, and he replied, "I think he went
to Whitewood to haul bales." The two officers left. This was said with
such a straight face that *I* almost believed it.

Contacts with Mounties occur only when there is "trouble." Indian cars and trucks are stopped routinely and searched for open
liquor bottles. Indians on the street who are obviously drunk are
hauled off to spend a night in jail, as are those who are rowdy
anywhere in town. The barkeeps do not hesitate to call the police
to arrest an Indian they believe is about to give them trouble. In
all these cases, the procedure is to release the offender in the morning, with a summons to appear in Magistrate's Court, held every
two weeks in the town hall. Standard fines are given—Indians always plead "guilty"—and Indians are usually given several weeks
to raise the sum. In the "police court" column of the Short Grass
News, which reports cases tried, the names of one or more Indians
appear without fail each edition, usually for liquor violations.

Scrapes with the law ordinarily take place in town, when the
police are called in by Whites. Police are rarely called to the reserve—not simply because there are no telephones there, but because Indians do not report one another to the Mounties.[12] As we
will see, "trouble" is handled in other ways. It seems, in fact, that
the police have little concern about reserve affairs, and that their
interest in Indians does not extend beyond the town boundaries.
As one officer put it: "We really don't know what goes on up there;
and we don't care very much, either, as long as they don't make
trouble in town." A favored drinking place for Indians—the "nuisance grounds," is several hundred yards beyond the town limits
and is not patrolled by the police.

[12] One man, who is something of a social outcast, does occasionally seek
assistance from the Mounties. When his house burned several years ago he summoned the police to investigate, accusing his brother. He also asked them to
patrol the roads during the 1967 Sun Dance, to make sure no liquor was brought
onto the reserve. Regarding him as a police informer, the other Indians hold
him in low esteem.

The stance that police take toward Indians is paternalistic, like that of other Whites. And they agree with other Whites about the sources of "the Indian problem." When I interviewed the local sergeant,

He was vague and guarded in his words to me, and seemed unwilling to make quotable, "official" statements. He said that the government may have made a mistake in giving drinking rights to the Indians [in 1961]. "I'm not criticizing the government, you understand. But," he explained, "with any privileges go responsibilities, and the Indians aren't willing or ready to handle responsibilities. You just can't give savages—I'm not calling *these* Indians savages—privileges and expect them to understand the responsibilities that go along. It simply doesn't work. They're bound to get in trouble."

Another (retired) officer gave his opinion:

The white man has not taken advantage of the Indians. It's really the other way around. We've helped them in every way possible since the beginning. I think we've helped them too much, so that now they won't do anything for themselves any more. Why should they? In the old days they were self-sufficient, and they took care of themselves. The old-timers never gave us any trouble. Oh yes, sometimes you saw a squaw drunk, but you could bet it was some cowboy who gave her a bottle. . . . Now, I don't know. . . . They don't seem to have any ambition; they won't do anything for themselves. They're all pretty lazy. They live from hand to mouth. They're not all of them bad, but most of them don't seem much good, either.

There is, finally, a slapstick quality to Indian-Mountie relations, as exemplified by the following incident. Janet Deersleep, an unmarried woman in her early thirties, had been sentenced by the magistrate to a month in jail on a number of counts, including petty theft. Since she was expecting a child, the magistrate allowed her to stay in the hospital and ordered that she would serve her time after the birth. A few days after delivery Janet asked a nurse for a pair of scissors with which to cut her hair, cut her way out through the hospital room's window screen, and escaped (the child was eventually given into the care of Janet's mother). The Mounties searched for her unsuccessfully on the reserve and kept an eye out for her in town. Several weeks later, she was spotted in town, and in the words of an observer:

You should have seen it. I thought I'd bust laughing. Janet took off across Front Street with two policemen after her and two others in a car driving around the block to head her off. She came back into sight a minute later with the same two after her, and they [the officers] were breathing hard. She headed into Ferguson's yard [a farm-equipment outlet], and they chased her all over the place ... under tractors and around swathers and reapers. [Officers] Green and Tylor were yelling, "There she goes ... over there ... you go around that way ... over here," and they looked like they were gonna drop. Finally Janet gets out the back and she was out of sight like a shot.

She was not caught until nearly a week later, and was then taken off to do her sentence.

It should be evident from what I have said so far that Whites are seldom present on the reserve. One rancher who had lived a mile from the reserve for forty years said that he had never been inside an Indian house.

The casual pace of reserve life is reflected in the informality of its leadership. Theoretically, a chief and three councillors are supposed to be elected for terms of two years. The lower offices are not filled at all, and that of chief is passed among the adult male heads of households, mostly to satisfy the Indian Affairs Branch. The chief has negligible authority and does not meet regularly with the band. When the rare decisions that affect the whole community are made, any action taken is the outcome of a consensus of the adult males. This happened, for example, with a resolution not to lease part of the reserve to a particular rancher. After a religious observance, all of the men talked the matter over for several hours and finally agreed that it would be better to have some of themselves grow fodder on the land. In these proceedings the chief's voice was no more prominent than any other.[13] This pattern of government closely resembles that of precontact times. Decisions concerning all the members of a nomadic Cree band were made by the assembled responsible males, after extensive

[13] Councillors' positions are not filled, and the position of chief is not actively sought, because Indians say that it is too much trouble to be chief, and that it puts a strain on personal relations to take a leadership role. As one man said, "Everybody thinks you're gettin' too big for your own good, and anything you say, people think you're gettin' bossy, tryin' to order people around."

debate and oratory. The chief then announced this decision to the remainder of the band; he did not have the authority to arbitrarily commit the band to a given course of action.

Leisure activities on the reserve are a mixture of traditional and modern amusements. With no set schedules for work and the routine of daily living, there are frequent opportunities to have fun. Indians enjoy attending "bingos" held in town, and are often to be seen at the movies. On the reserve, there are countless small gatherings to play cards, to listen to old people telling stories, or simply to visit and gossip. Sometimes impromptu "rodeos" are staged at the corral in the center of the lower camp: small boys are bucked off colts and attempt to lasso calves for the entertainment of an adult audience. The birthday of a child is occasion for its parents to throw a party, at which they are expected to provide a cake for the youngsters and wine for the grownups. In the summer a softball game may be held at any time. The whole band gathers, teams are formed of the young and old of both sexes, and play lasts until darkness makes it impossible to continue. Spontaneously, people will gather at a house to join in Indian songs, accompanied by drummers. Always, some of the best male singers are asked in turn to perform certain songs that they "own." If someone suggests a hand game, sides are chosen, and play may last through the night.[14]

It is not only in the realm of the unserious that traditional elements of Cree culture remain. To be sure, much has been lost: military societies no longer exist, bear ceremonialism is gone, and girls' puberty rites are not held. But a great deal has survived—most significantly, the Cree language. Several oldsters on the reserve speak no English at all, and children do not begin to learn English, as a second language, until age five or six. Very few Indians feel comfortable attempting to express themselves in this foreign language, and on the reserve only Cree is spoken, except when an agent or some other White is present. Moreover, every

[14] This ancient form of gambling involves guessing the whereabouts of a small token concealed in the hands of the opponent. It is surprisingly complex and is accompanied by highly stylized gestures and special gambling songs (Mandelbaum, 1940: 234).

person on the reserve has both a Cree name and a White name (see Chapter 6).

Indians are apprehensive of White medicine and doubtful of its efficacy. One woman I knew refused to let a doctor treat her broken shoulder and permitted the injury to heal improperly. Although Indian parents do take children to the clinic in town when they are seriously ill, traditional herbal remedies are commonly used for sick adults. Other forms of Indian medicine, both physical and ceremonial, also persist. Several band members know how to prepare "love medicine" and sometimes sell it to others. One man supposedly lured away the wife of another by this means, and the estranged husband of another woman had originally been attracted the same way. It is believed that the person toward whom such medicine is directed cannot resist its power and will be drawn irresistibly to the "magician." It is also believed, however, that this is dangerous business, and that misfortune may befall the user or some immediate member of his or her family.

At least a few Indians also know how to practice "bad medicine." These sorcerers are universally feared, and people, quite understandably, seldom talk about them. One sequence of events that took place several years ago is illustrative. Two strangers from another reserve appeared in Short Grass, and an altercation developed between them and several local Indians. One of the foreigners vowed revenge, and shortly before leaving town he claimed to have sent sickness to his enemy. However, the spell missed its target and came to rest on the victim's six-year-old daughter. A medicine man, called in from a distant reserve, performed a curing ceremony in which he "sucked" the intruded "medicine" (some porcupine quills) from the head of the child. Not long after, the child died, and the practitioner explained that he had not been called in time to save her. White doctors later diagnosed her case as a severe brain tumor.

The Short Grass Cree, in common with many other Indians, share beliefs in a number of less malevolent supernatural phenomena. Manitu, a single omnipotent entity, presides over a vast pantheon of lesser spirits who are believed to inhabit every living thing (Mandelbaum, 1940: 251–52). Any Indian can appeal to any of these forces for aid in some specific venture or for good luck in general, and on the reserve one often sees small bits of brightly colored cloth left tied to bushes as offerings to the spirit world for this purpose. The major religious celebration on the reserve, the Sun Dance, is similarly directed at the supernatural.

The Sun Dance, presided over by ritual specialists, is performed in order to place the community of humans in contact with the spirits from whom all blessings are secured, and is the outcome of a complex series of preparations stretching over many months (see Mandelbaum, 1940: 265–71). For the four-day ceremony itself, held each July, all band members contribute money for the food and gifts distributed to visitors, and all help to build the special dancing lodge, used only once. Supplicants vow to thirst and fast for one to four days during the ceremonies; they are obligated to dance the whole of each day and may not leave the lodge. Others help in drumming or singing to accompany the dancers, and help keep a fire going; and still others form an audience. Tents are pitched in a circle around the Sun Dance lodge, one for each family, and there are always a few tents belonging to visitors from other reserves. The Plains Indian Sun Dance has received great attention from anthropologists (see Goddard, 1917; Skinner, 1919). In Short Grass, as elsewhere, some details of the ritual have been dropped and others have changed, but the rite's importance has not diminished. The Dance has more than religious significance alone: it is equally meaningful as a reaffirmation of community identity, and it promotes a vital sense of solidarity among the participants.

So far, I have described in general terms some features of the Short Grass community, including the role of Indians isolated on the small, unproductive reserve, as a recognizably distinct subculture. Differences between Indians and Whites in values, styles of life, and relative position in the social hierarchy will occupy the remainder of this study. However, it is appropriate here to examine a few general similarities and differences between the Short Grass band and other Plains Indian communities.

There are, within a few hours' drive, much larger reserves to the east, west, and south of Short Grass, and I was able to visit a half-dozen of these, usually in the company of Short Grass Indians. The atmosphere of these places is strikingly different from that of Short Grass. For example, in 1967 approximately half the Short Grass band attended the Sun Dance at Rocky Boy, Montana. This was a large event, with thousands of Indian participants and observers, and more than a hundred tents were pitched around the Sun Dance lodge. There were concession booths selling food and drink, a gambling tent, and hand games in progress at all times. A Catholic priest had even set up a portable altar near the Sun Dance lodge for those of the audience who wished to make the observance a Christian one. Even though the primary purpose of the gathering was religious, the general attitude was festive, with much visiting between visitors' tents and houses on the Rocky Boy reservation; countless friends and relatives took the opportunity to renew ties and enjoy one another's company. There were also a large number of White tourists present—curious onlookers who had to be reminded constantly that picture-taking of the ceremony is not allowed.

By contrast, the Short Grass Sun Dance later the same summer was a small affair, with no White onlookers. Only a few carloads of Indians came from other reserves, and even these did not remain for the entire four days of the observance. There were only a dozen tents around the lodge (including my own), and no more than 20 people took an active part in the dancing and singing of the ceremony proper. There were no concessions or commercial ventures, and there was no gambling. The Short Grass Dance, in comparison with others, seemed a much more local, encapsulated affair, even though the details of the religious observance were virtually the same as those of others I saw.

The differences between reserves also show up with regard to powwows. Nearly every large reserve in Canada and the United States sponsors one of these annual secular gatherings, held during the summer and lasting three days or so. Again, the atmosphere is always festive: concessions, singing and dancing contests, prizes for best traditional costumes, and, of course, gambling and hand games. There is always a large audience of both Indian and White spectators at these affairs, and a great deal going on. At one powwow I attended in eastern Canada rock concerts were going on simultaneously with traditional competitions, and in the evenings there were concerts by well-known Indian performers of pop music. There has never been a powwow at Short Grass, and the band members seem content to attend those on larger reserves.

It is not only in ceremonial and social life that Short Grass seems backward in contrast with other reserves. There is little social and economic differentiation within the band, and dwellings are uniformly modest and small. On other reserves one sees housing ranging from what are essentially rural slums to modern, well-kept places. As one would expect, these bands include both households that are impoverished and some that are relatively well off, headed by men who have the skills to get well-paid jobs off the reserve or who have profited by using the reserve resources as individuals. In Short Grass, there are no marked differences between individuals in education, basic skills, wealth, or life-style. As I have indicated, this goes along with the absence of any visible leadership on the reserve. Except for the rotating position of chief, which brings no noticeable prestige or influence, there are no offices carrying any authority. Agents who come to the reserve must deal with individuals directly, since no single person or group acts as representative of the entire band. On most other reserves there are active band councils, and elected leaders manage the community's affairs.

In many Indian communities of Canada and the United States there are major splits between various groups—for example, between the White-oriented and the traditionalist, or between progressives and conservatives.[15] Such conflicts have a long history in Indian populations, especially since contact, and have often been drawn along religious lines. Sometimes the same community exhibits at least a three-way split, involving traditionalists, Chris-

[15] See, for example, Spindler's (1965) description of a large Blackfoot reserve in Alberta, where he was able to distinguish a number of types or categories of Indians, based partly on orientation to the White world. Bruner (1956) offers similar observations of a Mandan-Hidatsa community in South Dakota.

tians, and those who espouse some novel religious movement such as peyotism. No factions of any sort exist at Short Grass. There are, of course, personal feuds between band members, but these never lead to a division between ideologically opposed groups. Rather uniformly, Short Grass Indians neither challenge their subordinate position in the general scheme of things nor attempt to emulate their White neighbors.

Just as there is no split between factions supporting either acceptance or rejection of the modern world, there is no sign of any Red Power militancy on the reserve. As a group, Short Grass Indians have displayed no interest in joining Indian-sponsored movements intended to improve their lot. A leader in one Indian federation visited the reserve after the band had ignored repeated invitations to send representatives to meetings of his group. Ironically, his complaints were much the same as those of discouraged IAB agents: "They don't seem to want to do anything to help themselves," he said; "they just sit there listening, but never say a word." As we shall see, it is not that the Short Grass Cree approve of or passively accept their place in the social universe. But rather than seeking wholesale change, they have attempted to adapt to their circumstances in various ways, and to manipulate existing arrangements to gain personal and collective advantages. In later chapters, I will return to a more specific discussion of what it is they must adapt to, and how this adjustment is accomplished.

ON THE Short Grass reserve I passed many hours with an old Indian man, now dead, who patiently responded to my questions on kinship terminology, religion, and other matters, and who told me many stories of the days before White men arrived in his country. Often there were others present during these sessions, children and adults who enjoyed as much as I the old man's marvelous tales of spirits who presented themselves to men directly, of animals who spoke to humans, or of the fearsome, man-eating Windigo monsters. I asked him once if such things happened nowadays, and he said, "No, these things do not happen so much any more, not since the White men came and we gave away our land to them." Although he could not formulate it in words, he seemed to believe that Indians have, in effect, fallen from grace—that the spirits will perform no more miraculous deeds for Indians who have allowed themselves to be touched by the White newcomers. Nevertheless, much of traditional religious belief is still intact in Short Grass, and the Indians of the reserve have not forgotten the old days. It is necessary, then, to offer at least a brief account of aboriginal Cree life, and of some of the events involved in contact with Europeans.

The Cree were relative latecomers to the Northern Great Plains, arriving in the early eighteenth century to occupy territory previously held by the Gros Ventre and Assiniboin in the east and by the Blackfoot in the west. (The displacement of these groups and the movement of the Cree onto the plains have been well documented by Mandelbaum, 1940: 169–88.) Before, they had occupied a large territory near Hudson Bay in the country still identified with the "Woodland" Cree (see Jenness, 1932: 283–87). The earliest accounts, appearing in the records of Jesuit missionaries of the 1650's, describe the Cree as hunting and gathering nomads who spoke an Algonkian language. In the summer the tribes gathered in large lakeside encampments, supported by harvesting wild rice from canoes; in the winter, small groups moved inland to hunt in the woods (Innis, 1930: 143).

After the coming of the Hudson's Bay Company in the late seventeenth century the Cree became increasingly dependent on White traders for European artifacts and sometimes for necessities; fur-trapping began to take the place of food-gathering and hunting during some seasons (Mandelbaum, 1940: 170, 172). The traders also sent Cree deeper and deeper into the back country, both to hunt and to collect fur from other tribes, and they soon became middlemen in a flourishing exchange network (Innis, 1930: 93, 125, 156). Cree population, under the circumstances, increased rapidly. As the eastern streams were emptied of beaver, the Cree expanded westward along the northern edge of the Plains, displacing less well-armed groups. A desire for beaver and a reliance on subsistence techniques learned in the northern forests at first kept them in the woodlands (Secoy, 1953: 42–43). By 1730, however, some bands had begun to venture onto the Plains (Mandelbaum, 1940: 175). Initially, this was merely a seasonal occupation: after hunting buffalo for a few months, a group would return to the forests and trap lines for the winter (Innis, 1930: 143).

Gradually, some bands elected to remain on the Plains year-round, and there developed a marked sociopolitical division between Plains and Woodland Cree. By about 1825 there was a true Plains Cree culture, fully committed to the horse-gun-buffalo complex, which had discarded much of the cultural inventory based on a woodland environment. As other tribes to the west and south acquired both horses and guns, and as military patterns diffused, territorial boundaries more or less crystallized, and no one tribe was able to dominate or conquer another (Secoy, 1953: 59–63;

Stegner, 1955: 55). The most formidable enemy of the Cree and their Assiniboin allies was the Blackfoot Confederacy to the west. Against these, and against the Gros Ventre, the Dakota, and the Village Tribes of the Upper Missouri, the Cree engaged in perpetual horse-raiding and warfare. The Plains Cree themselves roamed through most of what is now southern Saskatchewan and part of Alberta. At the culmination of their westward expansion, shortly after 1860, they probably numbered about 12,500 (Wissler, 1936: 9); but by 1889 there were only some 7,000 and the same figure is given for 1940 by Mandelbaum (1940: 165).

Cree bands were loosely organized, varying in size and range over relatively short periods of time. There were at least eight major tribal divisions (Mandelbaum, 1940: 166). Eastern bands, such as the "Rabbit-Skin People" and "Calling-River People," hunted in the vicinity of the Qu'Appelle and Assiniboine rivers, sometimes spending part of the year in trapping (Denig, 1961: 118). Western bands claimed territory in the valleys along the North and South Saskatchewan and Battle rivers. All groups did not participate to the same extent in the horse-gun-buffalo complex, and the bands farthest west were those most dependent on the buffalo. Bands were named on a territorial basis, and each was integrated by common residence, by the wealth and prestige of its chiefs, and, to a lesser extent, by kinship (Mandelbaum, 1940: 221). Membership was not permanent, and individuals or families could transfer allegiance to another band when expedient.

Plains life seems to have required this fluidity at the expense of corporate cohesiveness (Oliver, 1962: 56), largely owing to the migrations of the buffalo herds. In the spring, Cree gathered in large encampments along the South Saskatchewan River, where buffalo were plentiful; in the summer, they followed the buffalo through the open prairie; and in the winter, they broke up into small groups as the animals scattered and retreated to woody districts. At all seasons of the year buffalo were available within the territory of each band (Mandelbaum, 1940: 189). It was the density of the herds that regulated the annual cycle (Oliver, 1962: 17): when buffalo came together in large numbers, so did Cree.

Seasonal movements and activities were largely determined by this pattern. In late June or early July large portions of a band, or perhaps several bands, encamped to hunt and to participate in the annual Sun Dance (Jefferson, 1929: 40–49). This was the period of concerted collective buffalo hunts, and the camps were maintained as long as buffalo were near. In autumn, deer and elk were hunted, and traps were built for buffalo. "If any of the tribe had been enticed by the Hudson's Bay Company to trap for furs, they struck out for the wooded places at this time" (Mandelbaum, 1940: 204). Since buffalo movements were unpredictable (Roe, 1951: 543–60), and the supply of meat uncertain, a given band might starve one winter and kill more than they required for the next. Many Cree collected at Hudson's Bay Company posts on the North Saskatchewan River during the winter months, begging or trading supplies against the dried meat and hides they hoped to secure the following season (Kane, 1925: 94).

Ewers (1955: 323–31), in a discussion of the Plains culture complex (Blackfoot), lists over a hundred associated traits—hunting practices, warfare, leadership, concepts of ownership, and so on. The Cree shared most of these. Horses were the source of prestige and wealth, and the economic basis of band integration. This was true even though the many eastern bands possessed relatively few horses as late as the 1850's. Perhaps one tepee in ten had a good buffalo-running horse, which made its owner rich and attracted less fortunate families as dependents. Since these animals were always vulnerable to raids from enemies, prestige on the Plains was never static.

Chieftainship among the Cree was informally constituted, and succession to chiefly status was not hereditary, although a son sometimes took over his father's position. There was no fixed number of chiefs in a band (Jefferson, 1929: 64), nor do there seem to have been tribal chiefs like those found among the Cheyenne. Essentially, the attainment of chieftainship was a matter of individual achievement and had no institutionalized procedure. A man who demonstrated valor in a battle, skill in hunting, unselfishness, and ability as an orator would gradually widen his sphere of influence and gain recognition as a leader. A renowned warrior, for example, would have acquired many horses in raids on his enemies, and would thus have increased his ability to obtain food and support dependents (Jefferson, 1929: 63, 67). But, although a brilliant war record was the single most important accomplishment required of a chief, other qualities were demanded. A chief was expected to be generous, to contribute substantially to ceremonials and dances, to feed and lodge visitors (Mandelbaum, 1940: 222). In this, he usually received some support from relatives, who provided him with objects of wealth to distribute in return for the prestige his position indirectly brought them. Gift-giving was also a means by which a chief could maintain peace, since he could assuage the anger of disputing parties by presenting them with horses or other valuables.

Though there might be several "chiefs" in one band, a hierarchy of rank was tacitly recognized among them (Mandelbaum, 1940: 222); and at council meetings one leader would outrank all others by seniority or by obviously superior ability. In any case, the degree of authority a chief had in his band was a matter of personality rather than ascribed status and was exerted mainly through informal councils. Whenever some decision was necessary, the chief's "crier" summoned the leading men of the band to discuss the matter, after which the chief would announce the will of the group's majority (Jefferson, 1929: 53).

Plains Cree bands each had a warrior society with prescribed duties (Mandelbaum, 1940: 224–29). A youth who showed promise and daring would gradually become recognized as a "worthy young man" within the band, though no specific obligations were attached to the status. Not until he was formally invited to sit in the warriors' lodge was he in a position to exercise authority, and this privilege awaited tangible evidence of his ability (Skinner, 1914: 518). Within the lodge, warriors were seated in the order of their prestige, the place of greatest honor going to the war chief, who was informally selected by the society. This office and that of band chief were distinct, although both were sometimes held by the same man. The authority of the war chief, however, was restricted to activities of the warrior society as a group.

Warriors, like band chiefs, were supposed to help maintain peace (Skinner, 1914: 520); and their societies were most active during the large gatherings, at which they supervised the movements of the camps and regulated collective hunts. When several bands came together for these affairs, each occupied an arc in the camp circle. Warriors' lodges were erected inside the circle opposite their respective bands, and there was friendly rivalry between the various societies, each boasting of its exploits and trying to outdo the others in display and dancing.

No individual hunting was tolerated as long as the summer camp held together. Everyone was required to remain in a single group while approaching a herd until the signal to charge was given by the warriors (Skinner, 1914: 523–29; Jefferson, 1929: 64–65), and the kill was distributed evenly among all participants. This gave the hunters with slower horses a chance to participate; otherwise, the few with the best horses would scatter the herd before others could reach it, and the collective kill would be small. The warriors punished a hunter who broke these rules by slashing his tepee or destroying his property. As was characteristic of many Plains tribes, this punishment was intended to reform lawbreakers and draw them back into the society. If a man took his punishment stoically, and if he committed no additional offenses, the warriors would contribute to the restitution of his losses after several days (Mandelbaum, 1940: 227), and sometimes he would even get more in return than the warriors had destroyed.

Whiskey Traders and Mounties

So far, I have emphasized the economic and social features of Plains Cree life that were most directly a part of the ecological adjustment the forest-dwelling Cree made to their new habitat. One must remember, however, that this "classic" Plains Indian adaptation lasted, at most, only about two generations. During this time an intricate network of mutual dependencies developed, involving the Cree and other Plains tribes, White trading companies, fur-trapping Indians to the north, half-breed voyageurs and hunters, and many other sociopolitical groups. The system as a whole extracted wealth—chiefly hides and furs—from the Plains with such intensity that the ultimate sources of that wealth were soon exhausted. New adaptive techniques were required all too soon, and previous ones, including those of Plains Cree culture, were discarded.

There were, of course, other reasons for the decline of Plains Cree culture—for example, the successive epidemics of smallpox that struck the Cree and other tribes for over a century (see Howard, 1952: 253–58; Denig, 1961: 72, 109). Still, it was primarily the disappearance of the buffalo, owing to overhunting, that paved the way for White settlement. The Plains Indians were not, of course, the only ones responsible for this. In particular, the Métis, or half-breed inhabitants of the Canadian frontier, systematically harvested enormous quantities of buffalo, as much for hides as for meat. By 1870 there were about 13,000 Métis in Manitoba and the Northwest (Howard, 1952: 336), and their way of life was neither Indian nor White. They borrowed adaptive techniques from both cultures, acting as both farmers and migrant buffalo hunters. In addition, they carried on most of the trade between Indians and Whites, at first by canoe and later over the prairies in the ingenious Red River carts.

As the buffalo disappeared from Canada, competition for the remaining herds became fiercer. The Hudson's Bay Company, to forestall American and other independent traders, built many new posts; and instead of awaiting the arrival of buffalo hunters at the forts, it began sending out trading parties that bargained for hides in the summer and wintered in the Moose and Wood Mountains or the Short Grass Hills. In spite of these measures, American traders from the upper Missouri continued to export a great proportion of the buffalo hides taken in Canada (Cowie, 1913: 187, 219, 357). They were not alone, for at the same time there occurred a great influx of buffalo-consuming Indians from the United States. These were mostly Sioux fleeing from military encounters with the United States Army (Sitting Bull crossed the line in spring 1877) and the policy of the Canadian government was to allow such refugees to remain as long as they were peaceful. In 1879 there were thought to be as many as 10,000 American Sioux hunting buffalo throughout western Canada (Roe, 1951: 478).

Under the circumstances, the destruction of the buffalo in Canada, begun in earnest in the early 1870's, preceded the final disappearance of the herds in the United States by several years and was completed before the opening of the Canadian Pacific Railway in 1880 (Roe, 1951: 483). The Plains Cree and the Assiniboin now found themselves thrown upon the resources of Canada's Indian Department. Starving, clothed in rags, and demoralized, they reluctantly quit the plains and began to occupy their allotted reserves in the north. One of the last parties of independent Indian buffalo hunters, however, gathered in the Short Grass Hills.

When Isaac Cowie had traded in these hills in the winter of 1871–72, the Hudson's Bay Company was no longer selling liquor to Indians, having given up the practice about 1860 (Cowie, 1913: 388). This offered a great opportunity to Métis and American-based traders, who had plenty of whiskey to exchange for buffalo robes. And Canada's brief "lawless frontier" era began when these rough and determined men pushed across the 49th parallel, ignored both Canadian and United States law, and erected trading posts. One of the most infamous of these, "Fort Whoop-up," was opened by two traders from Fort Benton in 1867 and conducted a lucrative, if tumultuous, business for about six years (Sharp, 1955). There and elsewhere, the traders prospered. "In one year, two whiskey posts in the Blackfoot country, now southern Alberta, sent nine thousand robes, worth about five dollars each, to Fort Benton" (Howard, 1952: 260). Indians murdered one another in drunken orgies, and there were frequent violent incidents between Indians and traders.

Sir John Macdonald, then Premier of Canada, secretly dispatched agents to investigate conditions in the Northwest, and their reports prompted him to suggest the creation of the Northwest Mounted Police in 1873 (Haydon, 1910: 12–15). The formation of this force was hurried along when exaggerated tales of a massacre in the Short Grass Hills filtered east. About a dozen White wolf-hunters from Montana had crossed into Canada in search of horses, which they were sure had been stolen by Indians. Inflamed by whiskey obtained from a Canadian post, they attacked an encampment of Assiniboin in the Hills, killing perhaps 40 with the loss of only one man.

In 1884, a column of 300 Mounties under one Colonel Macleod finally rode west to carry law and civilization to the Territories. Their overall orders were to patrol 300,000 square miles, inhabited by 30,000 restless Indians, but the whiskey trade was the immediate target. Fort Whoop-up and the other posts were destroyed, and those traders who had not fled in time were arrested and imprisoned; by the start of the new year, the whiskey trade was defunct (Haydon, 1910: 34–37).

During this period, the government pursued a policy of arranging treaties with the Northwest Indians. Buffalo were more and more difficult to find, and the Cree, forseeing the imminent arrival of White settlers, were willing enough to cooperate. Between 1874 and 1877 most of the Cree, as well as the Blackfoot, signed treaties providing for Indian reserves, a supply of agricultural implements, the establishment of schools, and annuity payments of $5 per Indian (somewhat more for chiefs). However, most Indians would not settle on reserves as long as there were still a few buffalo to be found on the Plains. At times, enormous crowds would appear at RCMP forts demanding annuity payments and ammunition so they could follow the herds south. And, as destitution and starvation grew increasingly commonplace among the tribes, the same scenes became a simple begging for food and clothing.

The RCMP fort near what is now Short Grass was for a short time the largest in the Territories—there were 103 men there, as opposed to 86 at Fort Macleod (Haydon, 1910: 89). The Mounted Police had their hands full maintaining peaceful relations between bitterly hostile Indian tribes, protecting work gangs of the Canadian Pacific Railway, frustrating the whiskey trade, and punishing horse thieves. The last problem was the most serious. Raiding enemy camps for horses was a Plains Indian institution that advancing civilization could not tolerate—especially when the horses were taken from Whites and Indians in the United States, or from the Mounties themselves. Although the Canadian and U.S. governments cooperated in trying to end raids by Indians in both countries, the practice was not curtailed until the turn of the century, and then only through an enormous investment of effort by the police. In 1896 the problem was tersely defined thus: "The country is so immense, and it is so hard to trace a man's property in horses and cattle, that this evasion of justice is quite easy" (Ann. Rept. RCMP, 1896: 4). Canadian Indians were worse off than American in this respect, since the Mounties were quick to enforce the law that forbade bringing stolen property across the line. American Indians, not so restricted, found it much easier to capture and keep horses from Canada.

Early Days at Short Grass

As early as 1865 a few Indians and Whites had realized that the buffalo were in danger of extinction. Nevertheless, as Jefferson recalls (1929: 37):

When the treaty was first made neither white man nor Indian ever dreamed that the buffalo would disappear overnight, as it were. All was done on the assumption that hunting and farming would go hand in hand till the new life was as familiar as the old; when, therefore, the whole native population was suddenly thrown on the Government's hands, no provision had been made for such an emergency, and ... it is not difficult to see by how narrow a margin the Indian in those days escaped starvation.

Settlement on the reserves began as soon as the treaties were signed, but at first only a few bands moved to their new homes. Since the Cree had no knowledge of farming, the government did not force bands who could support themselves by hunting to give up their nomadic life; and only half of the 23,000 treaty Indians in western Canada were on reserves in 1881.

By 1883, however, it was clear that armed bands of Indians could no longer be permitted to roam the Plains. More and more settlers were entering the Territories, and their horses and cattle would be vulnerable to Indian raids as long as the Indians had complete freedom of movement. This was one of the most convincing arguments for the abandonment of the Short Grass fort in the early 1880's. While the fort stood, Indians had a meeting place and a source of supplies when they could not find buffalo. Moreover, their habit of gathering in large numbers at a point so close to the international border meant that horse-stealing raids between Canadian and American Indians would inevitably continue, causing trouble for law-enforcement agencies on both sides of the border. The Commissioner for Indian Affairs in the Northwest Territories wrote in 1884:

I look upon the removal of some 3,000 Indians from [Short Grass Hills] and scattering them through the country as a solution of one of our main difficulties, as it was found impossible at times to have such control as was desirable over such a large number of worthless and lazy Indians, the concourse of malcontents and reckless Indians from all bands in the Territories. Indians already on their reserves will now be more settled, as no place of rendezvous will be found where food can be had without a return of work being exacted, a fact which tended materially to create much discontent among those who were willing to remain on their reserves, as well as to increase the laborious duty of our agents.

By 1882, the Canadian Pacific Railroad had reached the Short Grass region, and a shantytown had sprung up on the future townsite. The police then decided to build a permanent post at the same location, using materials salvaged from the abandoned fort. This decision was in part influenced by the imagined threat of Indian revolt. And shortly afterward a small band of roving Cree demanded provisions from the railroad gang, telling them they had no right to cut timber for the railway because the land belonged to the Indians and not to the White man. The frightened contractors retreated to the police post and insisted that the Indians be dispersed. Local settlers, too, were apprehensive of these "homeless" savages, and every missing head of livestock was reported as killed or stolen by Indians (Ann. Rept. RCMP, 1885: 9). The police, under pressure from the Indian Department, began the task of herding the Cree north. In 1884, the Commissioner of the Northwest Mounted Police wrote: "There are now, I am pleased to say, no Indians at . . . Short Grass."

Nomads were not the only Indians to suffer. The first permanent building in the area had been established in 1879 as the nucleus of a cooperative Indian farm some three miles from the present townsite. In accordance with government policy elsewhere, the Short Grass establishment was assigned an instructor whose job was to teach the Indians agriculture. Early reports credit this effort with gratifying results. Altogether, more than 100 acres were planted in corn, wheat, and vegetables, and the abundance of early harvests led the White instructor to predict that the Indians living near Short Grass would soon be self-sufficient. The Indians, too, were encouraged by their success, and were annoyed that there was not enough seed available to plant even more land; in the meantime, farming income was supplemented by the sale of ties to the CPR (some 4,500 were cut in 1881). But promising though the venture appeared, the Indians working the farm were also moved in 1884, owing to the tensions already mentioned, as well as to the government's desire to keep a comfortable distance between the Indians and the border (Ann. Rept. Indian Affairs, 1885: 204).

Thereafter, no treaty Indians lived near Short Grass. However, a small band of nontreaty "stragglers," led by the chief Foremost Man, resisted every effort to remove them from the Short Grass Hills, and more than 20 years passed before any regular assistance was given them. The members of this band were the ancestors of many of the present residents of the Short Grass reserve. At one time, Foremost Man's followers numbered over 500; but some were persuaded to join other bands already settled, and others drifted into the United States, until little more than a hundred remained in 1885. The survivors camped in the hills, began to construct log cabins, and attempted to put in a crop of potatoes, with no implements other than a single spade. The presence of this band was disconcerting to new White settlers in the area, and on at least one occasion they persuaded the Mounties to search the camp for weapons.

Foremost Man, insisting that he had been promised a reserve in the hills near Short Grass, refused to leave the area. His band soon gave up the idea of living by farming, and began to subsist on local game, which the RCMP superintendent complained was in danger of extinction—even birds' nests were robbed (Ann. Rept. RCMP, 1887: 31). Buffalo bones were gathered and sold for shipment east, where they were used as fertilizer. The Indians also polished buffalo horns and peddled them to travelers on the CPR at the Short Grass station; on some days, individuals could earn as much as $8 in this way. As western Canada was settled, however, the Short Grass band found increasing employment in agriculture. Because their labor was cheap, White settlers slowly grew better disposed toward their remaining around the town; and shortly after the turn of the century the Indians were joined by some Whites in their requests that a reserve be established near Short Grass (though the government persisted in trying to place them on reserves elsewhere).

Two types of economic relationships gradually crystallized between Indians and settlers: the seasonal employment of Indians by Whites, and the permanent residence of an Indian family on a White ranch or farm. Small-scale ranchers needed help in the fall to harvest and stack winter hay, and also hired Indians to dole out feed to cattle over the bitter winter months. Less work was available during the spring and summer, so that many of the Short Grass Indians did not give up the generations-old pattern of spring and summer nomadism. With the buffalo gone, however, these wanderings were more aimless. Single families would roam the hills in search of small game or would visit with relatives on other reserves; and in the spring many band members would travel to reservations in the United States to attend the Sun Dances there.

The casualness of the Indians' life renders historical research difficult, at least for data since the turn of the century. There are few published sources, and accounts by Indians themselves are rather sketchy. The following excerpts from a brief oral auto-biography given me by a 50-year-old Indian man are a fair illustration of the material one must work with:

I can't remember much before I was seven years old. Things have changed a lot in the last twenty years—the Indian's life, I mean.

We used to haul wood into town—that time we used wood in town. I was about ten years old, I guess, about '28 or '29. We used to use horses; it would take six hours to take a team to town. We used to camp for the night, then in the morning we'd cut up the wood for burning. We did this year-round. We used to charge one dollar a wagon load. We went sometimes with my dad, sometimes with my mother's dad, sometimes with my mother, or Shortie or Joe [brothers]. We buy some stuff in the store—everything, sugar, butter, flour. Everything was cheap that time. That time Father was live this place. Lived in a tent. We had log house that time like this, too, but we used tent when we went to town. Stay sometimes two nights when we finish selling wood.

My father he was cuttin' posts, tryin' livin' that time. That time there was no help at all [government relief]. I think my old grandfather was workin' over here—we call 'im that Gus Andert—but he died. He worked for 'im twenty years, eighteen anyway. Haul hay, help plowin', everything; feed cattle winter and summer. He [Andert] live there eighteen years, had three [Indian] girls live with him, and some boys. My dad was one of 'em.

There was no school then. Old Indian fellas didn't want us to go to school in town. Old folks was afraid we would go to war then. That time was war, 1919. I guess lotta Indians went that war—lotta Indians kill 'em up east. Young fellas, they learn to read they go into Army, that's what the old fellas afraid.

There was lotsa Indians that time, more than now. All pull out around '28 or '29, '30 I think. They can't live very much; this place no good, no work, long ways to town, that'sa reason. Round 1916 there was a big flu here, too, and in town. Lotsa Indians, they die then. Lotsa White mans die too.

We was pull out from here. Left 1936 with my old dad and mother. We went Moose Mountain. At that time die my old grandmother. My mother's mother died in the States when we were at Rain Dance, same spring died that old fella. Lived there about two years. After that two years we come back from Moose Mountain. That time was 1940. We don't like that place, water no good, lotsa sickness. No good place.

In 1942 died my old mother; so we scattered all over. We tried workin' here, workin' all over the place. My father got married again in '41.

That's his own sister-in-law. No more kids with that lady. He met her Moose Mountain, she Jimmy's wife. He went back there again that year and married her. I went then too.

About '39 I start ride horses in stampede. I rode all over. Last time was '57 up here in Greenfields [a famous amateur rodeo in the hills]. Then I quit. I made maybe $140 the whole time. I rode bareback and saddle bronc, and wild-horse race. That's all I ride.

I was start bronc-riding that time, '39, when I met wife that time over Moose Mountain. Live with that girl there. I was stay with that father-in-law. Had a kid about one year later. Wife catch cold and die pneumonia in that winter—that was about 1940. Then I come back here. The baby stayed with that grandfather. Indian Agent ask me sign paper so that baby stay with old folks. He was supposed to stay there and come here when he 21, but he din't do it. I think he married now, but I don't know when. See him five years ago, when we went down Moose Mountain for Sun Dance, in 1958.

So I come back here by myself. I stay with Dave [friend], and we cut posts, we live that way. Was huntin' a little bit deers and coyotes. I live with that Dave until 1942. He die 1953. For while I work for old George Carson. Nice guy; he treat us pretty good. His wife nice woman too. We start at seven o'clock and quit about five o'clock evening—right time to work and right time to quit. They didn't work us too hard.

But then I was bronc-ridin', so I went east maybe two, three weeks. We work out winters, maybe sometime spring, summer. Then we go ridin'. Lotsa work then, but no more. I guess the ranchers got lotsa machinery now; they don't need no man now.

There seem to have been several different trends in Indian-White relations over the past seven decades. Initially, as we have seen, the Short Grass Whites were somewhat fearful of Indians. One old-timer relating his memories of his family's first days in town, just before World War I, said:

That first night in town we stayed in Anderson's house in town, hardly more than a shack. After dark, we heard the Indians start singing and drumming over in the flat, and it sounded real spooky. They kept it up all night, and none of us got a wink of sleep, we were so sure that they were going to murder us in our beds.

Another woman described an encounter shortly after her marriage to a rancher:

Pete was gone, out feeding the cattle one afternoon, and three really mean-looking Indians came to the kitchen door and asked for food. I gave them a little and they asked for some more, and when I said I couldn't spare it they got real nasty and made threatening gestures, and I tell you I was scared. But I didn't back down, and they went away. When Pete got back and I told him, he laughed, but he said it was a good thing that I stood up to them. Not that they would have hurt me or anything, but they will *try* to intimidate you, and if that works they'll never stop pestering you.

At this time (up until the depression), Indians were also regarded as exotic, objects of curiosity. One rancher relates:

We kids used to sneak up to the Indian camp and lay on our bellies out of sight just to watch 'em. They probably knowed we was there, but they never let on. They usually just ignored us. But we would lay there for hours just watchin' them; watchin' the squaws cuttin' up gophers, or tannin' hides and makin' clothes, and the Indian kids playin'. We never got tired of spyin' on them like that.

Up to the beginning of World War II, Indians were employed more or less steadily by Whites. One rancher reported a regular pattern for Indians working on White ranches. In the spring, Whites would buy the log dwellings in which Indian families had wintered, using the materials for fenceposts. Indian families would camp on ranchlands (if they were not away at other reserves), and the Short Grass reserve itself would be practically deserted for the summer months. Much of what was transacted between Indians and Whites at this time was not on a cash basis: for example, an Indian family might do some fencing for a rancher in exchange for slaughtered beef and some grain. And a store that operated near the reserve until the early war years did most of its business by barter. Indians also did cut firewood, which they could easily sell in town for a dollar a wagonload.

Relations between the two groups seem to have been marked by little overt tension. Indian and White children played together (they do not today). There were "fiddle" or barn dances attended by Indians, and White men (though not women) attended dances on the reserve; several Indians could play the violin and were much in demand at these get-togethers. There were also some community practices that have since died out. For example, it was customary at Christmastime for Indians to visit Whites house-to-house in town, receiving various small gifts (this still takes place on the reserve itself, among Indians). At this time, as one rancher pointed out,

Everybody was poor, we was all in the same boat. Winters was bad, and we all had a hard time scratchin' out a livin', especially in the Depression. You wouldn't believe what mom used to make our kids' lunches out of. And them poor buggers [Indians] would come around to ask for some grease and flour, and mom would give 'em whatever she could, which wasn't very much. *Then* they was always willin' to work for their food; they didn't just ask for handouts. And you could trust an Indian's word, too, better'n some White men. . . . Like I said, we didn't have no problems, except the problems that we *all* had together, tryin' to stay alive.

The idea persisted, nevertheless, that Indians were something less than human:

They'd eat *anything*. I remember once we had this pig that died, we didn't know what of. They came around while it was still lyin' around and getting putrid, and asked my dad if they could have it. He said to take it and save him the trouble of buryin' it, and I'll be damned if they didn't have that thing cut up and ate before you knew it. And it didn't seem to hurt 'em one bit, either.

After World War II, however, Indians were increasingly isolated from the White community. As the economy stabilized, and as farm equipment became more readily available, manual labor was less in demand. There had been a small community at Greenfields, about a mile from the reserve, in which there were a school and the small store/post office already mentioned. Owing to the difficult winters on the "bench" and to a pattern of out-migration and the consolidation of small ranches into larger ones, this community gradually dwindled and disappeared. The last family sold out and moved to Short Grass in 1964. At present, there is only one occupied ranch within easy walking distance of the reserve.

PART TWO

The Preservation of Self

FIVE   Self-Sacrifice

THE SUBJECT of this book as stated earlier has to do with the adjustment of Short Grass Indians to the fact that their moral worth is denied by Whites. Now I wish to take up the problem in detail, and to examine closely the sorts of evidence Whites grasp to confirm their conception of Indians as profane persons. To begin with, we must have some idea of the behavioral and value domains within which Whites and Indians gain knowledge of one another. By behavioral domains, I mean the specific settings of interaction —the pubs and cafes in town, jobs on ranches and farms, and so on. By value domains, I refer to certain areas of life in which clusters of characteristic behavioral proscriptions and prescriptions operate, and in which self-attributes are communicated by one's relative observance of these standards. In the main, I will discuss issues having to do with work, money, privacy, and leisure, since these are important to the community members themselves; they dominate gossip, and in them are to be found the standards by which people evaluate one another.

First, let us be sure we understand the general characteristics of situationally appropriate (or inappropriate) comportment. In streets and other public places, or in settings where interaction between persons is shielded by barriers to perception, things can and do go wrong, in the sense that anomalous information is communicated about people present or about the situation. Occasionally we find our persons or clothing in disarray in view of others; our attention can wander from a conversation and require retrieval; and sometimes we find ourselves party or witness to an unpleasant scene. Intentionally and not, people will commit faux pas of varying degrees of gravity; and when such events occur, there is general awareness that something inappropriate to the situation has happened. Whether or not corrective measures are taken (e.g., in the form of sanctions applied to the offenders), information has been presented that gainsays the relevant definition of situations and situated selves. In all of these cases some situational propriety has been violated.[1] Rules that govern people's interactional behavior, though not always easily formulated by those involved, become evident when they are broken. Quite obviously, one can discover a great deal about what ought to happen in a stream of events by studying situations that develop when these expectations are not fulfilled, including the manner in which various kinds of hitches are dealt with.[2]

The structure and composition of situations within which people's involvements are regulated vary considerably. Perhaps the least consciously structured are those in which people are in one another's presence and mutually visible but are not engaged in any joint venture, as is true in most public places. Interaction takes place insofar as information is communicated, and social distance is cooperatively maintained, even between people waiting at the same bus stop. In general, conduct is guided by rules requiring that persons not behave in bizarre, threatening, or otherwise offensive ways that might signal some illicit or unoccasioned involvement. A typical lapse in this requirement on the part of one Indian occurred one Saturday in the Short Grass movie house:

Oscar Lodgeskins entered, obviously drunk. He groped about for a seat, found one, and promptly went to sleep. The audience half filled the theater. The movie, about the French Foreign Legion, continued for

---

[1] This chapter leans heavily on Goffman's work on communication conduct, especially as outlined in his *Behavior in public places* (1963a: Parts II–IV).

[2] In anthropology, interest in "trouble" and in the ways its occurrence reflects an inexplicitly formulated set of rules has been widespread, particularly in the study of primitive law. See, for example, Llewellyn and Hoebel (1941); Hoebel (1954: 29–45); and Gluckman (1965: 169–215). For a description of "normal trouble" in one sort of public place, see Cavan's observations on "bar behavior" (1966: 67–87).

about a half-hour, when the first bloody battle took place: a number of mounted Arabs attacking an outpost were noisily being beaten off. The din awakened Oscar, who, noticing the dead and dying, began loudly to sing, "Aiee......" He (apparently) thought he was watching a Western battle between Indians and Whites and began a death song (though it's doubtful if any of the audience realized this). At first, there was silence, and then, after perhaps a minute, a few sniggers among the audience, followed by loud (and somewhat nervous) laughter. Oscar became aware of this, muttered something in Cree I couldn't hear, and curled back up in his seat as the battle came to a close. "Another crazy Indian," I heard a woman sitting near me say.

Untimely involvements can occur in almost any context. On a late afternoon in one of the Short Grass pubs,

Wilbert Antelope sat with us for awhile, not saying anything, then moved to a table in the corner by himself. He was clearly preoccupied, and also a little drunk, but not rowdy. He began to cry. Jimmy Deersleep went over to him and talked with him for a minute, and then returned, explaining to the rest of us that Wilbert was thinking about his mother (who had died a couple of months previously). That was why Wilbert was crying. The rest of us, the group of Indians at the table, went on talking as before, leaving Wilbert to his private grieving. His weeping was, however, apparently unacceptable to a waiter, who went to Wilbert's table and said with some pique: "Look, Wilbert, if you're gonna sit here and slobber I want you outa this place."

People not only attend to their private business in public, but also initiate contacts in which they become implicated in some joint activity. This can be a fleeting and impersonal event, such as asking and receiving directions from a stranger, or a more protracted and intense one, such as arranging a party for close friends. In both cases the conditions under which engagements may be initiated are subtle and complex.

In Chapter 1 some reasons why people do or do not wish to engage in interaction were discussed. To involve oneself in activity with another may be viewed as potentially profitable; but it may also be threatening, physically or otherwise, particularly if the other is a stranger with unknown motives. There is a basic difference in the openness of one's stance toward the acquainted and the unacquainted.

One might say, as a general rule, that acquainted persons in a social situation require a reason not to enter into a face engagement with each other, while unacquainted persons require a reason to do so. In these two rules, the same general principle seems to be operative, namely, that the welfare of the individual ought not to be put in jeopardy through his capacity to open himself up for encounters. (Goffman, 1963a: 124)

Thus one should maintain a certain accessibility or openness to overtures from others, at the same time preserving a circumspect wariness of possible injury or exploitation. Conversely, a properly comported individual does not rudely force himself upon others.

It appears that the balance of interaction is less delicate in rural communities like Short Grass than in urban centers. Short Grass is a relatively isolated, "particularistic" community in which few newcomers settle and in which people recognize one another on sight. An adult member of the community may or may not know the name of someone he sees on the street, but he will be able to identify the person as a local and is likely to nod at him or greet him verbally. Similarly, people know a great deal more about their neighbors than is usually the case in a middle-class urban setting. Gossip accounts for part of this, and there are other sources of information: a glance at the weekly newspaper reveals who has been hospitalized and why, who is receiving out-of-town visitors, who has made a weekend (or even overnight) trip to Cross Point, and who may have been fined for a minor liquor violation. Similarly, the fact that strangers can be identified at once means that they may well be asked their business in town, politely and after a cordial greeting. In large urban communities, by contrast, people are open to engagement with others by virtue of the position they occupy (such as policeman or salesman), because they are "open persons" like children, because they are "out of role" (as when an ill person is approached with offers of assistance), or because they are acquaintances. And, of course, the openness of persons to overtures from others differs from one sort of interaction setting to another: "idle" conversation permissible between strangers in a supermarket checkout line is less so in a funeral parlor.

Although a diffuse ethos of informality prevails in Short Grass, regulations concerning the opening of engagements with others still exist, creating the possibility of infractions. For example:

John Bullrobe was standing on the corner (in front of the post office) when a rancher came down the street toward the main entrance. John turned to face him and said, "Hey, wait a minute, I want to talk to you." The man looked straight ahead and walked briskly by John, ignoring him. John began to follow, until the man started up the steps, when John gave up the pursuit and the attempted contact, returning to his post.

Once an encounter is under way—when the opening moves have been made and acknowledged—further rules come into play, including those that close off the engagement to others nearby. And just as unengaged individuals control information flow between themselves, those engaged control information exchanged as part of the engagement. A certain loyalty of participants to the engagement (and in part to the wider setting) is assumed. They are expected, for instance, not to talk so loudly as to call the interaction to the attention of bystanders. Conversely, one should not appear to attempt overhearing or otherwise penetrating an engagement to which one is a bystander. This naturally involves a certain cooperation between participants and bystanders—the former attempting to modulate their interaction within the encounter so that it is possible for the latter to respect the privacy of the engagement.

The problems arising when bystanders are admitted to an existing engagement are somewhat like those created by the potential (but sometimes indeterminate) accessibility of lone individuals in making and accepting overtures. And again, the nature of the situation is all-important: it is one thing to approach a conversational knot at an informal party and quite another to do so with strangers in a restaurant. A perceived trespass of engagement boundaries can all too easily occur, as happened on a Short Grass sidewalk one weekday morning.

Frank Pope and I, on the way to the Moon Cafe, were stopped by George Dixon in front of the dimestore.... George wanted to discuss arrangements for cooperatively hauling winter hay. Sam Timber sauntered toward us, with the obvious intention of entering the conversation, perhaps to make some request. His appearance was ignored by Frank and George. . . . Instead of standing off a bit until his presence could be noted, Sam came right up and began to speak. . . . George said, irritably, "Can't you see we're talking? What do you want?" Sam said, "Oh, nothin' . . . just gonna say 'hi,' " and continued on down the street.

Obviously, there is a large assortment of interaction situations for which convention apportions the nature and degree of involvement by participants. The number and specific content of rules vary, as well as the extent to which their infraction meets with sanction. However, a few very general features seem common to all situations (Goffman 1963a: 193–97): regard for gatherings is expressed in the maintenance of communication boundaries by both participants and bystanders; participants preserve an appropriate degree of attentiveness, not permitting their attention to stray to irrelevant matters within the engagement or to external concerns; and participants moderate the intensity of their own involvement. These proprieties serve to keep rein on the self, and to communicate the image of a respectable social self.

All this is simply to say not only that our behavior is under scrutiny, but that performances are judged by standards or rules governing the minute as well as the gross effects of that behavior. As an illustration of how fine such judgments can be, Short Grass Indians are criticized by Whites for matters so seemingly trivial as eye contact and talking. I often heard the complaint that "Indians won't look you directly in the eyes when you talk to them." And indeed, Indians characteristically deflect their glance to the ground in casual conversation with Whites. (It is also interesting that Indians commonly wear sunglasses in town, where Whites seldom use them.) To Whites, this action is a sort of evasiveness that they find objectionable, and it renders Indians suspect; also, it is probably a major reason for the stereotype of Indians, in Short Grass and elsewhere, as taciturn and wooden-faced.

Talking is a similar problem. Except in certain contexts, such as in a pub after a few beers, Indians seem to Whites singularly uncommunicative. One rancher said to me: "Hell, you can't get 'em to say a word unless they're plumb drunk; they just stand there and act stupid." Keith Basso, in an article on the Western Apache (1970: 227), suggests that Indians remain silent whenever they feel that social relationships in a situation are uncertain. I suspect that this is also true among Short Grass Indians. But for whatever reason, it is true that Indians do not ordinarily converse freely with Whites (though they do so with ease among themselves); they will not exchange small talk, or even respond readily to direct questions. As Whites see it, they have "clammed up," revealing a major deficiency in interpersonal comportment.

Shiftless Indians

For Short Grass Whites, the positive value of work and its corollary of self-sufficiency occupy an exalted position among the normative standards by which they judge themselves and others. To be regarded as hard-working is to receive the praise of the whole community. I met, for example, a childless couple who managed a modest ranch in the hills alone under most difficult conditions, including being snowed in for three months of the year. Being able to make a go of it with no help was a source of pride for them and the object of frequently expressed admiration by others. Two maiden sisters also ran a ranch alone; and although they were regarded as eccentric for never having married, they were nonetheless ungrudgingly esteemed. "You gotta hand it to 'em," one rancher said; "they can take care of themselves okay. . . . I seen 'em work harder than lots of these young kids we got around here." Another 56-year-old rancher, talking about his life and accomplishments, boasted, "I never took a single penny of relief once, an' we went hungry plenty of times." He continued:

I came to this country forty years ago with nothin' but what I was wearin' . . . and there wasn't no kind of work I was scared of, and I took some pretty miserable work, too. Then I took this place on shares [i.e., he managed another man's ranch for a share of the profits, and gradually bought him out over a period of twenty years]. . . . I never buy nothin' that I can't pay for right there on the spot. There ain't a thing on this place that ain't paid for, not a tractor or truck, not even a pin. And you can bet that there ain't a place in town where I couldn't get credit or a loan on my word alone, except I wouldn't take it, ever. . . . I tell you, if I was your age today I'd have the world by the tail. When *I* started out it was a damn sight tougher than it is today. Hell, I'd start out $100,000 in the hole and still make it if I was 25 years old. . . . A lot of these kids whine and whimper and say they can't get work—there's plenty of work around, just cryin' for someone to do it. The trouble with them is they won't touch anything they don't think is fit. . . . I'd hate to count up the tons of cow shit I shoveled when I was their age.

In fact, rural life near Short Grass is strenuous, even though there are seasonal breaks (for example, in midsummer, between calving and haying times). Fences and machinery require constant attention, and the work required to maintain a herd or a mixed farm is back-breaking. During calving time, men may stay up day and night with their animals, taking only occasional short naps. There are also roundups, branding, and—perhaps the most strenu-out task of all—cutting, bailing, and hauling hay for winter fodder. And then men must go out in severe winter weather to locate and feed their cattle. Because of the innumerable small tasks that require attention, most ranchers have no time for vacations; at most, they can take no more than one or two days away from their property at a time.

The woman's share of the family labor is likewise arduous. Except for the more prosperous enterprises, most ranching families near Short Grass live off the land to a great extent. Gardens are kept by the wives and require constant watering and tending during the arid summers. Women milk cows daily, make their own butter, and sell excess milk to a dairy cooperative. Most households keep chickens and other fowl, as well as pigs. Many families make their own sausage—and the mustard to eat with it—and nearly every ranch wife I knew made her own bread and preserves, frequently on a wood-burning kitchen stove. Particularly during the busiest periods, women are up before their husbands, around 4 A.M., and retire after them, their chores yet unfinished. Women are also more isolated and tied to the household than men. The wife of the veteran rancher just quoted at length was able to visit town only a few times during the winter, and no more than once a week during the summer. For her, to spare the time for a permanent in a Short Grass hairdresser's was an extraordinary luxury. A hard-working wife is a necessity to the family business, and she receives commensurate moral approbation from the community.

Townspeople, though their work may be less physically demanding, place a similar emphasis on "taking care of yourself" and on diligent labor. Independent shopkeepers work long hours with a minimum of paid help, and salaried employees frequently hold several jobs. It is not unusual for, say, a gas-station attendant to work as a barman in the evenings. In any event, and aside from the real extent of one's labors, the idea of constant toil as the sole honorable means to success—the familiar Protestant Ethic—is widely shared and explicitly verbalized by Short Grass Whites.

It is commonly believed that Indians do not measure up to these prized standards. Many Whites with whom I talked, including those who had been on the reserve, were convinced that Indians do nothing there but "sit around." One woman characteristically remarked:

What do they *do* up there all the time? . . . I think I'd go crazy if I sat around like they do all day long, doin' nothing. From what I can tell, they got it easy. . . . Don't do a damn thing. *I* wouldn't last a week with nothing to do. . . . You know, before the Fosters sold out and moved to town [from a ranch near the reserve], Rachel [Foster] used to have Oscar Lodgeskins' wife, Lena, come to help her with the house. Of course, she had to teach her everything, how to clean house and so on; but Lena learned real well and sure was a big help. You'd think at least that *she'd* know better and do something to keep her own place up . . . after all, she knows how. But from what I hear, the place is a pigsty. . . . I wouldn't touch a cup of tea in that filthy house.

To a certain extent, of course, these observations are not unfounded. On the reserve there are fewer imperative demands on one's time, less work to be done. Indians have but a few cattle, and no agricultural equipment needing care and repair, although they do attempt to put up hay for winter feed. Except for occasional hunting, they do not live off the land to any great extent; and their summer nomadism precludes the tending of chickens or vegetable gardens. Fenceposts are cut to earn extra cash for individuals, but the reserve community as a whole does not have the land, machinery, or technical knowledge to engage in intensive farming or ranching. One exception, already mentioned, illustrates the difficulties faced by Indians in attempting "self-help," and the ways in which Whites judge their efforts.

Johnny and Gordon Antelope, both in their early thirties and married, had secured 15 impregnated cows through the IAB, intended as a nucleus for a herd of their own. Gordon left his job with the highway department and moved from town into his former house on the reserve. He had managed to save a little money, with which the two bought a used hay mower and a small, ancient tractor, which they stored in a nearby log shed once occupied by their father. Unfortunately, they forgot to drain the radiator for the winter, and the engine froze and was ruined. In the early spring, with the last of their savings, they bought a replacement tractor and a small truck; the IAB helped them acquire a used baler.

The two worked to attach a small corral and animal shelter to the log building, and in mid-April the cattle were delivered. With some luck, all 15 had calved within a month. Though some calves were sick in the beginning, all were healthy and doing well at the time I left in the fall of that year (1967). The brothers, however, were plagued with equipment failures. When we began cutting hay in July, the mower failed, and the job had to be finished with old-style horse-drawn machines. The baler, an ancient and rather exotic model, also refused to work. The instruction manual gave us no help, nor were the Antelopes able to persuade the dealer from whom it had been purchased to come to the reserve to service it. In the end, the loose hay had to be loaded onto the truck with pitchforks for transport to the shelter.[3]

To support a cow and calf for the winter, approximately two

3 No assistance was offered by reserve members, other than the men's father. The prevailing sentiment was that the Antelopes were getting "too smart," that is, were somehow putting themselves above the others. Other Indians felt the IAB "shoulda given us all cattle, not just them two.... What's so good about them?" Nor did the brothers seek the assistance of neighboring White ranchers: they felt that they could afford neither the share of their crop that would be expected nor the time it would take to pay for assistance in kind.

tons of hay are needed—that is, about 30 tons for the Antelopes' small herd. Toward the end of haying time, after countless truck-loads of unbaled hay had been moved, only about half that amount was stored. One day, as we worked, a local rancher passing through the reserve stopped to check the progress:

(To Johnny, who was resting): "You still haven't got that baler fixed up?" Johnny replied negatively. The rancher, after a pause, said, "Say, who taught you boys to make up a haystack, anyhow? You got it all wrong. You gotta make it thicker at the bottom and taper it up. . . . First big storm comes along's gonna blow your hay all to hell an' gone." He shook his head disapprovingly, side to side, and commented to no one in par-ticular, "You gonna need at least fifteen, sixteen tons; looks to me like you got only six or seven." All through this, the Antelopes said nothing (their father was there, too, helping). When the truck was empty and ready for another trip, the rancher climbed in his pickup to leave, adding a parting observation: "You boys ain't gonna make it to Christmas. . . . They'll just be a lot of dead beef up here . . . (laughing) But at least they'll be some meat for you to eat this winter, hey?"

Later, I heard this man report the visit to another rancher, in a tone of great amusement. Both agreed that "if it wasn't so comical, it'd be pathetic." The general attitude of the White community was that the whole project had been incompetently managed and was doomed to failure, and that the young Indians did not have the determination to see the job through.

As another requisite of self-sufficiency, Whites consider it neces-sary that one's property, including animals, be well cared for; and in their judgment, Indians do no better in this regard. Ranchers often complain that the band, despite insistent prodding, refuses to keep its fences in repair, with the result that cattle stray from both sides. One group of ranchers gave up demanding that In-dians repair a cattle guard and did the job themselves, billing the IAB for materials and labor. Criticism is liberally offered concern-ing other kinds of property. A retired rancher, living in town, claimed:

That bunch don't take care of anything, *anything*. They just don't seem to care. They can take a perfectly good old truck and drive it into the ground in a week. You can't get anywhere doin' like that. . . . And ani-mals! They'll come into town in the winter with a team and wagon when

anybody else in his right mind'd stay put. I've seen it too many times:
they'd see one of the others or somebody passin' in the right direction
[in a car or truck] and stop 'em for a lift, and just tie up the team to a
fence at the side [of the road] and leave 'em there.... Why, last week
or so, Frank Pope cut loose a team that'd been tied up for two days, an'
it was more'n 20 below! John Bullrobe's, I think they were.

Another rancher said:

I don't know how many times I've cut hobbles off Indian horses [a rope
tied between the forelimbs to keep a horse from straying]. They'll tie up
an animal like that and leave him that way for days, or even weeks, so
they can catch 'em easy. They all do it, even in the winter, and I don't
know how the horses keep from starvin'! John Deersleep, he's the worst
of the lot.... I cut loose one of his team last winter, and the poor animal's shanks were all torn up.... That's no way to treat an animal
at all.... He came down to my place mad as hell, wantin' to know if it
was me that done it. And I told him, "You're goddam right it was me, and
I'll do it again every time I see an animal hobbled up like that, whether
you like it or not."

The remarks of a man whose ranch adjoined the reserve represent
the views of most Whites with whom I discussed the subject:

Alex Lewis (speaking to Bill McIntosh and me) told us how George
Antelope stopped him in town, wanting to make a deal to borrow a
hayrake from him. Alex said, "They got two rakes up there from the
[Indian] agent five years ago, and never used 'em once ... just let 'em
rust. You think I'd lend 'em mine the way they treat equipment? Not on
your life! I turned 'em down." (I asked—or remarked—that those were
horse-drawn rakes, and inefficient.) "Listen," Alex said, "I did up a lot of
hay with a team in the old days.... You'd be surprised how fast you can
work with one—*if* you don't mind a little work, that is."

The idea that Indians are lazy, and that idleness marks daily
life on the reserve is, as I have said, widely shared by Whites, and it
is sometimes communicated openly to Indians, as the following
incident indicates. Near the reserve, an annual "stampede" is sponsored and run by a Short Grass roping club. In 1967 the stampede
area, with the animal pens and chutes, was in need of repair, and
neighboring ranchers and farmers had begun fairly extensive reno-
vations. Among the few men who were doing most of the work,

there was concern that the project might not be completed in time, and several days previously one of them had gone to the reserve to solicit volunteers. No Indians had shown up, to the workers' resentment. "Hell, it's their stampede too," one man said. "They don't mind comin' for the fun, but they won't do none of the work." Another man claimed that he wouldn't trust any of them with "a measuring job or any fine work," but wanted their help with the menial tasks. Later, two young Indian men did appear, but apparently more out of curiosity than anything else.

Chester set them to work tamping dirt down around fenceposts, a task that they accepted with obvious reluctance, and which took them out of carshot of the rest of us who were working on the chute gates. As the two walked away, George said in a stage whisper, "All you gotta do is mention work, and you scare 'em away like rabbits." The two pretended not to have heard.... They stayed for about a half hour at this isolated task, and finally wandered off toward the reserve. Dixon, pointing with his thumb over his shoulder, said sarcastically, "See, what'd I tell you!"

Indians are believed to be unreliable as well as lazy, and thus make undesirable hired hands. Many ranchers now refuse to hire Indians at all, and others will do so only when no other help is available. One man complained:

You know I hired Gordon last month to help with the haying.... I had him working the rake and I left him alone to do it. Oh, it worked okay for about a day and a half, and then Gordon comes down to the place and said that the towbar on the rig was busted and he had to stop. He asked me for ten bucks and said he'd get back to work when it was fixed. Now I *knew* the sonofabitch busted that machinery on purpose, just like I knew he would head to town and the beer hall like a shot with the money.... I couldn't prove it, but I'm damned if I'll trust him alone with my machinery again.

An Indian is paid around $10 for a day's work helping to haul bales, although ranchers do not like to pay them a day at a time, fearing that they will not return to work. An Indian man and I were helping one rancher with haying, and the Indian requested his pay after a day's work. The rancher told him that he didn't have the money with him and that he would pay later, but at length was persuaded to give the worker a dollar "on account." After the Indian had left, the man said: "I could of given him the money, but he'd make a beeline for town and the pub, and that'd be the end of it. . . . I'd have no help tomorrow." More often, pay is simply delayed until the entire job is done.

Another rancher, with whom I stayed awhile, worked out a simple but ingenious solution to the problem. An Indian man who was helping him would not be paid daily; but each evening after supper he was given a bottle of wine (the cost being deducted from his wages). He would then retire to the barn to consume it and sleep. The rancher explained to me: "If I gave him his pay before the weekend, he'd disappear to town and that'd be it. But I made 'em promise not to tell any of the others I was doin' that. . . . If it got out on the reserve that I was giving him even a little to drink, why there'd be a party every night in the barn, and I won't have that."

The belief in Indian shiftlessness was similarly expressed by a shopkeeper in town:

[In an interview] I suggested that with occupational training perhaps some of the young men might become self-supporting. At first, Wilcox agreed with this, but then decided that this is just an "excuse," that training and jobs *are* available, and all that is required is for Indians to show the initiative to go after them. Wilcox saw this as part of a set of "excuses" on their part, including what he identified as their attitude that the White man owes them a living. He also expressed the conclusion that the Indians' ties to and dependence on the reserve community prevented them from facing the real world responsibly. Charity had made them lazy, shiftless, and aimless. . . . We talked about Bighorn and the fact that he had lost a job due to repeated absences. . . . Wilcox said: "They've got no discipline or responsibility. Sure, lots of young White kids goof off now and then—play sick for a day to get off work so they can go for a swim or something—but they outgrow it after a while, they develop a sense of responsibility. . . . And at least they make up some kind of a story to tell you [like feigning illness], and even if you know they're fibbing, you can let it pass and get 'em back to work. . . . But these Indians just don't bother to show up—no explanation, no nothing."

Thus to a charge of generalized irresponsibility is added the further accusation that Indians do not even show the courtesy of providing the "white lies" that make it possible to pass over a disruption smoothly.

It is indicative of the prevalence of these ideas among Short Grass businessmen and merchants that not one I questioned said he would hire an Indian man or woman, even for the most menial of tasks. Irresponsibility was not the only reason cited for this—included were standards of cleanliness, honesty, and so on. One grocer said: "The trouble is, if you wanted to give a job to one of 'em, the others would soon show up to pester him for money or something, and the place would get to be a regular hangout. . . . They wouldn't *let* him work in peace as long as they thought they could get something out of him."

Whites universally attribute the laziness and irresponsibility of Indians to the existence of relief payments. It is maintained that the laziness is a recent development, and that things were otherwise only a few decades ago. A man who had sold his ranch near the reserve and retired to town recollected:

There were just as many Indians around here [in the 1920's] as there are now, except that they supported themselves then. . . . They sold firewood and posts, and worked on farms. They trapped and hunted a lot . . . they don't do that any more. The women tanned leather and did beadwork, and the men polished buffalo horns and sold 'em. For five bucks you could get a real nice deerskin shirt with beadwork designs on it that musta took some squaw months to make. They were *real* Indians then. Now, they don't do nothing . . . just sit back and wait for their checks to come in. They don't have to do anything; why should they? . . . If the government just took 'em off relief and they started to get a little hungry, then you'd see 'em make an honest living like the rest of us.

As a consequence of this view of Indian character and performance, when Whites do employ Indians, those hired are generally watched closely and supervised almost constantly. Before paying Indians for stacking bales of hay, for example, a rancher will inspect the job carefully to see that it has been done properly. The same is true of an Indian who stacks fenceposts he has cut on the lot of the lumber dealer to whom they have been sold; on one occasion, an Indian who had not completed this job before closing time was refused an advance on his posts and was not paid until he finished the next morning. A rancher related another typical incident to my wife:

Bill paid a short visit, and we talked about the "sing" on the reserve on May 21. He seemed interested to hear that they were keeping it up. . . . He said he knew that sweet grass is used in their ceremonies. He told me about a time when John Deersleep and Dave Antelope were working for him at harvesttime and he had gone out to check on them. They were crawling around on their knees, and he went over to see what they were doing. They said that they had found a spot where sweet grass was grow- ing, which they said was hard to find, and they were picking it so that it could be braided and burned at a ceremony. Bill said that he didn't mind that they took the grass, only that they did it on his time. He said, "I told them that now that they knew the spot they could come back *after* work and pick it. . . . I wasn't gonna stand for them picking sweet grass when I was payin' 'em to make hay. Those fellows seemed to think they could do anything they wanted to as long as they stayed in the field."

The "idleness" and unreliability of Indians are also established in contexts other than work situations—especially in town, where the band members are, in White eyes, invariably seen to be "loiter- ing." It appears to be a widespread and general rule in Western society that one should not only be engaged in some legitimately identifiable activity when in the presence of others, but should also *demonstrate* an involvement in some situation at all times, even if this is merely journeying somewhere or awaiting some- thing. What one does, then, shows others that one has a purpose (Goffman, 1963a: 58–59); and a person whose involvements and intentions are not apparent is always suspect. Even a pastime as trivial as window-shopping is preferable to a lack of discernible involvement.

In Short Grass, there are certain times when these requirements relax, and an air of aimlessness prevails. On Friday afternoons and evenings, especially in good weather, the two-block business sec- tion of the town is crowded with persons strolling, chatting, or standing singly or in small groups. This is the time when families come to town to shop, pick up mail (there is no rural free de- livery), and transact business with townspeople; and when these tasks are completed, it is usual to relax on the streets or in the cafes, in a markedly convivial atmosphere.[4] People wander in and out of the Old-Timers' Museum, a shoe-repair shop that contains a large collection of Western memorabilia, and other public places. Children, left to their own devices, weave through the adult traffic, or are sent to the movies while their parents socialize in one of the cafes. But even at these times the presence of Indians on the streets, though less conspicuous, is still singled out. I once heard a woman say to a companion, as a large knot of Indians passed, "Looks like the natives are restless tonight."

At the other extreme, there are times when loitering on the downtown streets almost automatically arouses suspicion: on Sundays, when all stores are closed and people are expected to be involved in family pursuits; on Mondays when most stores are not open; and, of course, late at night. However, both Indians and Whites are usually elsewhere under these circumstances. Perhaps the most conspicuous time for Indians (or any person, for that matter) to be seen loitering is on weekday afternoons and evenings, when those in the streets and public places are expected to be there on business, or at least to be en route to some legitimate activity. Even at the lunch hour, there are relatively few people about on weekdays; and Indians who visit Short Grass then complain that they may be told to "move on" by the police, asked not to stand in front of business establishments, or informed that they have overstayed their time in a cafe. Their problem is to appear to have some purpose, and they try to do this in a number of ways.

Indians tend to avoid places where their presence has no apparent purpose—banks, the more expensive shops, the power company, and so on.[5] Instead, they frequent the lobby of the post

[4] There are fewer people in town on Saturday, since the banks are not open then and one cannot combine business with pleasure. However, the pubs always seem more crowded on Saturday than on Friday, which seems more a "family day."

[5] An instructive incident occurred when I bought a used tire from an Indian man to use as a spare and gave him a check in payment. He returned several hours later, saying he had tried to cash it at four places in town where I was known and had cashed checks previously, including my bank, and had been refused at all. As I have already mentioned, no one on the reserve has a savings or credit account in Short Grass.

office, several filling stations, and a small secluded park at the edge of the business district. These are all relatively "open" places: that is, unless information to the contrary appears, it is assumed that people in a post office, whatever their economic and social status, have business there, or that someone sitting in the park is simply resting before moving on. None of these places are oc-cupied for very long, however. For example, I knew one Indian man who habitually visited the post office several times daily, since a good command of a relatively busy intersection could be had from its windows; but he never remained more than about 20 minutes, knowing that the postal clerk could be counted on to shoo away Indians who remained longer. Another way to avoid the appearance of idleness is to keep moving, to seem to have business somewhere. And when the same man left the post office, he always strode off purposefully down the street. For similar reasons, an-other Indian seldom appeared in Short Grass without a worn (and usually empty) briefcase, which added a more businesslike flair to his travels about town.

Of course, it is possible for Indians to spend a substantial amount of time in one of the pubs, or in a local cafe. But they often lack the money to stay in such a place for very long, and in any case their presence is conspicuous and is open to the same condemnation it would receive on the street: on a weekday, one should be working at something and have business to attend to other than drinking or gossiping. In actual fact, few White ranch-ers or townspeople are to be seen in the pubs on most afternoons, and none of the proprietors involved are anxious to give their establishments the reputation of "Indian hangouts."

A more congenial spot, at which Indian men spend greater lengths of time, is the town pool hall. From its window one has a fairly extensive view of traffic on the main street, but passersby cannot easily see into the dimly lit interior. In this way, one can idle away the hours without publicly appearing to do so. In a few other places, mostly alleys or farm equipment lots, the traffic pat-tern or the placement of large objects affords a similar one-way perspective, and Indians invariably gather. Between 6:30 and 8, when the pubs are closed, one can generally find a group of Indians at the "nuisance grounds" on the edge of town. Other favored spots are near the tracks of the Canadian Pacific Railway, and at the house of a Métis woman who is friendly with, and related to, a number of Indians.

All these are places where time can be passed unobserved, since people appearing in town openly on weekdays are supposed to be engaged in some sort of purposive business. One way that Indians further minimize their visibility, which can give them away as loiterers, is to negotiate the town by using its alleyways. It is possible, for example, to get from the post office to the pool hall or the liquor store, and from these to the park, enclosed by bushes, without ever being seen. At times, there seems to be an entirely divided traffic pattern in the town, with Whites going about their business on the streets, in plain sight, and Indians pursuing their interests through the alleys.

Some of the difficulties encountered by the idle, and the conflicts that can develop, are shown in the following incident, which also points to some differences in the experience of Indian men and Indian women. The pool hall and filling stations are acceptable places to loaf, but they are exclusively male domains and are not open to either White or Indian women; nor could unescorted women enter the pubs until quite recently. When the men are in one of these places, or during inclement weather, there are few places in Short Grass open to Indian women (although they also spend time in the post office and the park). One solution attempted while I was there was to take refuge in the town laundromat, and for several months Indian women were frequently to be seen there, sitting for long periods in the chairs reserved for waiting customers. The patience of the woman caretaker of the place wore thin, as recorded by my wife:

On my last visit to the laundromat the attendant spoke to me for the first time, inquiring about what my husband and I were doing in town. She said, "People have been asking me about you," and it became clear that she was the nexus of a wide gossip network. . . . Once our connection with the Indians was established, she told me that she wasn't going to let any more Indians come into the place, having decided on that policy the previous day. Expecting then that they would come around to sit when the beer parlors closed, she locked the door at 6 P.M., putting up a sign that it would be closed from 6 to 7. At 7, she returned to open up, to find a White man impatiently waiting and angry about the irregular closing time (he had left clothes in the drier), and an Indian woman who tried to "slip in," whom she blocked, telling her she wasn't wanted there. She added that the man caught on immediately to what she was trying to accomplish by closing, and gave his approval.

She aired (to me and three other women present) her complaints about the Indians: they got the floor dirty; they sat around drinking, not doing any laundry. She accused them of throwing empty bottles into the back yard, and said that when there was a "bunch" of them there they smelled, and decent people wouldn't come in. She related how a couple of weeks ago she came in to find Janet Deersleep there, "sleeping off a drunk," and called the police, who arrested Janet and took her to jail. She expressed thorough disgust with the Indians, and wondered what possible interest they might hold for anyone to study.... She continued to talk to the others present, and elicited approving agreement from them.... One woman said, "I don't blame you a bit," and commiserated with the attendant about all she had "taken" from the Indians. Another woman said that she had seen Indians in town, and the attendant said, "Well, if any of them come around here, I'm not lettin' them in." ...

When I was finished and ready to leave (about 4:30), Violet Antelope, Margaret Russell, and another Indian woman I didn't know appeared in front, and looked as if they were going to enter the glass door. They opened the door, looked in, and saw the attendant. Not a word was said by anyone, but icy stares were directed at them for a tense couple of seconds, and Violet let the door close, and they all left. When they had gone, one woman said indignantly, "You'd think they'd know better; they know they're not welcome here any more."

The key issue with regard to Indians' perceived idleness, whether on the reserve or in town, is not so much that they do nothing but that their inaction does not reveal their intentions, which are therefore suspect. When they are present, and especially when they are not demonstrably involved in some legitimate activity, Whites fear the worst—that a situation may be disturbed, or that they may be exploited. A good example of this is the failure to establish an Indian "friendship center" in town: White church and town officials were openly of the opinion that even a legitimate place for band members to loiter would soon become a spawning ground for illegitimate activities. Much of the Indians' own reluctance to enter many public places in Short Grass, it would seem, stems from an awareness of this suspicion. They rarely enter the more exclusive shops, the cafe frequented by the more affluent Whites, the hotel lobbies, or the hardware store; and when they do, the reaction to their presence is distinctly unsubtle. For example, one dime store in Short Grass uses a self-service system, with checkout counters, and has a salesroom in the basement; this is usually unattended, but Indians, unlike Whites, are followed down to it by a salesperson.

In the stores, of course, it is the Indians' probity that is suspect. Most White residents of the community at least question the honesty of Indians, and some are convinced of their inherent dishonesty,[6] even though Indians are very seldom caught stealing— during fourteen months the only such case I recorded was that of a child who took a toy from a general store. The relevance of this attitude to the kinds of places in which Indians do or do not present themselves can be indicated by examining a single retail establishment.

Carver's, a prosperous Short Grass clothing store, specializes in Western garb of fairly high quality, catering to those who seek to fill the cowboy image. It is not patronized by Indians. As one Indian woman put it, the salespeople are "too snotty." Shortly before the Sun Dance, my wife and I accompanied two Indian couples on a shopping tour to the nearby city of Cross Point to buy cloth (both to offer to the spirits during the ceremony and to make new dresses for the women). While the women were shopping the men and I went off to have a beer and "look around." Among the half-dozen stores we entered was the Cross Point branch of Carver's, where we looked at clothing and leathergoods. John Bullrobe spent some time looking over a display of fancy Western

---

[6] For example, ranchers near the reserve often expressed unease about making family excursions to town, for fear of leaving their places unattended and unprotected from Indians. I heard of one rancher who, convinced that Indians were stealing from his freezer, left in it some meat "doctored" with a cattle medication that was "sure to make 'em shit their brains out."

belt buckles and finally made a selection; but we browsed a little while longer before leaving.

What was notable during all this was an absence of the "shyness" that had characterized exchanges between the same Indian men and the Whites in Short Grass. In talking with salesmen, my companions were self-assured and direct in a way I had not observed before. In turn, they (and the women during their shopping) were served promptly and courteously in a way they would not have been at home; and they were not, in Carver's or elsewhere, watched suspiciously as they examined merchandise. Among the reasons for this was that Cross Point has very few Indians living in or near it; consequently, the city lacks Short Grass's "Indian problem," and its residents do not display the degree of wariness of Indians common in the smaller town.

Mendicant Indians

Just as Short Grass Whites esteem industry, self-sufficiency, and independence, they consider thrift an important personal attribute. Ranchers and farmers, who receive most of their annual income from a single yearly sale of cattle and crops, must exercise great care in planning the next year's expenses and in stretching their financial resources. They deplore extravagance and consider such things as equipment purchases carefully, often patching up old equipment to "squeeze another year out of it." In fact, a majority of Short Grass ranchers and farmers manage their enterprises quite conservatively, "refraining from excessive investments and innovations, preferring to live simply and accept modest returns" (Bennett, 1969: 127). It is not surprising that Indians' behavior with respect to money excites the amusement and the disapproval of Whites as much as their use of time and care of property do.

Many Whites I interviewed, as indicated earlier, believe that the band could be self-supporting and that the incomes of individual families are in fact adequate: "It may not look like it," a farmer said, "but they make plenty of money, cutting posts and everything." A rancher who was better acquainted with individual Indians than most other Whites reported:

Before relief started they used to cut more posts than now, but they still cut quite a few. Of course there's not too many left on the reserve . . . they ain't what you'd call conservationists. I know they cut posts off the Forest Preserve, and they cut posts off *my* land too. You just can't trust 'em. . . . If you start to cut a stand of timber [off your own land], you got to finish the whole thing, or they'll finish it for you. . . . I was talkin' to Oscar Lodgeskins the other day, and he told me that so far he's made 18 trips to Beecher [a nearby town] with 200 posts a load, and that he's been getting 16 to 19 cents apiece for 'em. I figured it up, and it comes to around 250 dollars. . . . That ain't so bad for the little work they do. But he hasn't got a damn thing to show for it. Nothing. . . . No animals or machinery, not even clothes for his kids. He just pisses away the money as quick as he gets it on silly things—mostly at the liquor store. He told me that last time they didn't even make it back from Beecher with any money. But they had a good time, okay.

To Whites, then, Indian profligacy is but another form of a pervasive irresponsibility. Events and transactions that seem to confirm this are common. For example, one afternoon in a pub a middle-aged Indian named Louis Scarbelly ran out of money after drinking beer for an hour. He approached several White acquaintances to ask for loans and was abruptly refused. Finally, talking to a rancher who was also in the act of refusing, he said loudly, "Well, I'll sell you my truck." The vehicle, a 10-year-old Chevrolet half-ton, was battered but otherwise in good running order, and Louis asked $40 for it. The rancher, sitting at a table with several others, began to bargain jokingly with Louis, who was in earnest, offering him 50 cents. As prices were exchanged and claims and counterclaims were made about the worth of the truck, Whites at other tables began to listen to the fun, grinning at one another.

After about ten minutes of this the rancher said, in mock seriousness and with a wink to bystanders, "I'll give you five, and that's it." Louis answered, "Make it seven." At first surprised, the rancher took seven dollars from his wallet and passed to it Louis, who handed him the key, at which the man said to his companions, "You saw that; that was fair and square." Louis left the pub, accompanied by much laughter from the bystanders. "I'll be a son-ofabitch," the purchaser said. "Why, the goddam spare tire is worth that much." Another man's remark, greeted by laughter, was: "You notice how he wouldn't go below the price of a gallon of wine, and how quick he took off outa here?"

The story of the transaction quickly circulated around town (I heard it repeated three times the same day). And it was told not only as a source of amusement but as further documentation of the lengths to which Indians' irresponsibility could go. Several days later, Louis sought out the rancher and asked to buy back the truck, finally agreeing to ransom it for 100 posts (worth about $20). The rancher's decision to return it was probably influenced by Louis's revealing that he had neglected to mention an outstanding lien of $200 on the vehicle when he parted with it.

The attitudes of Short Grass Whites toward what they see and hear of Indians' money management can best be illustrated by following the course of a particular relationship between one rancher and a young Indian man. Although the relationship itself was unusual, the issues and problems encountered were not.

Tony Dumont, the son of an Indian woman and a Métis man (and in his mid-30's at the time of my fieldwork), was unemployed and alcoholic. It was not unusual for him to be drunk for days and sometimes weeks at a time. Although he periodically swore off liquor, his abstention never lasted very long. He was married (though not legally) to a woman nearly ten years his senior, and lived with her and their four children in her house on the reserve. Tony's mother had died when he was a small child, and he had lived with various relatives on the reserve, although his father was not entered on the band list. Apparently, when his father was in the district working for Whites their relationship was not a good one, and Tony suffered harsh beatings. Today, although Whites who know Tony express affection for him, he is thought of as a "hopeless case," an Indian who will not realize his potential. He is personally most engaging, with a whimsical sense of humor and an imaginative facility with English. Though he does not read or write, he speaks more fluently than any of the Short Grass Indians. Drunk, he is given to extended monologues of self-hatred and despair.

"*I sometimes think about it, think that maybe the White man treats us like he does 'cause he don't understand us, and that's too bad. Some other times I think he does understand us, and that's worse.*"

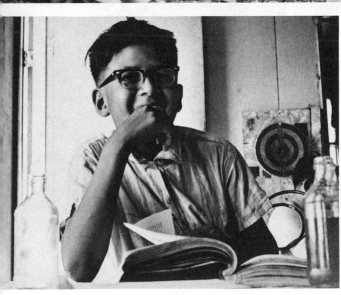

"Cree children almost always receive demonstrative affection and permissiveness. . . . They are free to play, eat, and sleep as they please, and they are included in nearly all adult activities."

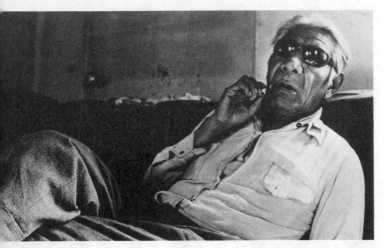

*"Except in certain contexts . . .
Indians seem to Whites singularly
uncommunicative."*

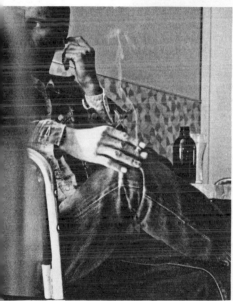

"The 'idleness' and unreliability of Indians are also established in contexts other than work situations—especially in town, where band members are, in White eyes, invariably seen to be 'loitering.'"

"Many of the 'old ways' remain.·... Much of Indian culture is intact."

The Stampede

When Tony was 18, he left the reserve to take a job with a fairly affluent rancher who seemed to have taken some interest in his welfare. The ranch was more than 20 miles from town, and Tony had little contact with other Indians for several years. When he was about 20, he received a legacy of some $1200 from a distant relative on another reserve. Though admonished by his White employer to save the money, Tony left his job and "signed off" the band list—that is, gave up his legal status as an Indian and thus acquired the right to purchase liquor. As Tony and others described the next few months, he and his friends lived "high on the hog." He bought a used car, which was soon wrecked, and went through the money "as fast as we could spend it."

His money gone, Tony asked for and received his old job back. But his reinstatement did not last very long: there were incidents of machinery damaged while he was drunk, long lectures and promises not to drink, repeated incidents. Finally his employer, concluding that Tony was incorrigible, fired him. During a drunken spree shortly thereafter, he stole another man's car and wrecked it, for which he was arrested, tried, and sentenced to a year in prison. After his release another rancher, Frank Pope, took Tony under his wing, intent on helping him make something of himself. Pope built a small house on the ranch for Tony and his wife, and took over the supervision of the Indian's finances:

I started him off at $140 a month, and he was making $200 when he left. We'd sit down and try to put him on some kind of a regular budget.... We'd figure out what he owed, pay the bills, and set aside money for groceries. We even started a savings account for him at the bank; that got up to $280 before Tony finally blew it. For a while there I had him on a once-a-month payday—he could get through that long without asking for money.

Frank's tutelage extended to matters other than financial:

Once Tony's hand developed some kind of an infection on the skin. I took him to the doctor's.... It was probably the first time he'd seen the inside of a hospital in his life. But we went, and I paid for it out of his salary (but I increased his salary that month). I even got him to get a health insurance card.... He'd never had one before, never hung onto his money long enough to get one. . . . We used to sit up late at night drinking coffee and talking about all sorts of things—you know, life, and how to get ahead. I even started giving him reading lessons, but he gave up on that after a while.

Tony's drinking problem continued, and at first he and Frank went to the pub together. Frank's ranch, closer to town than Tony's previous employer's, was the scene of numerous parties, attended by Indians who were attracted by Tony's (and Frank's) financial resources. There were recurrent misadventures during this time, until Frank finally persuaded Tony to attend meetings of Alcoholics Anonymous in Cross Point. As Frank put it: "I told myself I was going in order to get Tony to go, but I guess I knew that I needed it just as much. . . . I was afraid it'd reach the point where I'd be drinking with 'em on the reserve, and I'd wind up with my name in the police court column. . . . I didn't want to shame my family." But Tony's attendance was short-lived, and after a brief respite he was again "off the wagon." Frank, however, continued to go to AA meetings, and Tony's unreliability became increasingly intolerable to him. Tony withdrew all his money from the bank, overturned one of Frank's trucks during an unauthorized trip to town, and could be counted upon less and less to help with the chores. Finally, with Tony himself convinced of his unworthiness and Frank of his unsalvageability, Tony and his wife returned to live on the reserve.

Tony is somewhat ambivalent about his present status. He will sometimes speak critically about "those Indians up there," as if he were not one of them, and at other times refer to himself as a "dumb Indian." Living on the relief money his wife receives as a band member, he is sensitive about his presence on the reserve and acts so as not to offend anyone, not wishing to be asked to leave. For example, he never speaks at the irregularly held council meetings but remains quietly in the background. He knows that since he is no longer a band member, his presence on the reserve is technically illegal; and he once remarked to me bitterly that he could be charged with trespassing while having supper with his family in his own home.

Frank Pope thinks he has learned a lesson from his association with Tony and vows never to hire an Indian again on a full-time basis. He remains friendly with Tony and sometimes employs other Indian men temporarily; but he regards his attempt to "teach an Indian responsibility" as a failure. Many Whites who know of his experience agree. As one man put it, "I never would have put up with the crap Tony dished out to him. . . . I think he was crazy even to think he could get anywhere with Tony or any other Indian." Interestingly, Frank attributes his failure to his inability to break Tony's dependence on the band and free him from the influence of the other Indians.

The reason Tony doesn't mind jail is 'cause it's a lot like living on the reserve. . . . You don't have to make any decisions, just do what you are expected to do. The same reason I didn't mind the army. . . . I also think he'd be better off without Margaret [Tony's wife]; she is so tied to the reserve and the old ways. He was always a better worker at the times she was in the hills . . . and I told him even then that he should leave her and go live a hundred miles from the nearest Indian.

Thus, in their transactions with Indians and from their observations of Indian behavior, Whites conclude that no Indians possess the desirable qualities that define responsibility. They do not save money or plan ahead, they are "impulsive," they lack self-reliance, and they are spendthrifts. Whites even go out of their way to gather evidence of this. One man made a point of checking up on the purchases of Indians at the grocery store whenever he was there: "You should've seen them. I watched everything that went through the checkout. . . . They [an Indian family] had all sorts of fancy things: imported ham, strawberries, soda pop, candy . . . things I wouldn't even buy for myself. No wonder they wind up hungry at the end of the month. I guess they figure it's all free anyway."

Perhaps the greatest gulf between White "values" and those of Indians is found in the Whites' insistence on the equation of work and money, and in their rejection of "getting something for nothing." This was clearly exemplified in one encounter between an Indian man and a Short Grass housewife. The Indian, George

Antelope, has only one eye, and ordinarily wears sunglasses to conceal this. However, he appeared one afternoon at the woman's door, without his glasses, and asked for $2 for gasoline to get back to the reserve. Smelling alcohol on his breath, the woman proceeded to give him a lecture instead of the money, scolding him and insisting that if he had not spent his money on drink there would have been no need to beg. "There is one thing I absolutely will not do," she told him, "and that is give an able-bodied man money."

Trespassing Indians

I wish now to examine one further selected area in which Indians are seen to transgress the rules that guide behavior among Whites—in this case rules that concern what might be called social space. In Chapter 4 I mentioned the phenomenon of social distance, particularly as this affects the transmission of information about the self. Embodied in this is a pervasive rule of behavior:

When persons are mutually present ... it is possible for one person to stare openly and fixedly at others, gleaning what he can about them while frankly expressing on his face his response to what he sees. ... It is also possible for one person to treat others as if they were not there at all, as objects not worthy of a glance, let alone close scrutiny. ... Currently, in our society, this kind of treatment is to be contrasted with the kind generally felt to be more proper in most situations, which will here be called "civil inattention." What seems to be involved is that one gives to another enough visual notice to demonstrate that one appreciates that the other is present (and that one admits openly to having seen him), while at the next moment withdrawing one's attention from him so as to express that he does not constitute a target of special curiosity or design. (Goffman, 1963a: 83–84)

Civil inattention requires that persons strike a balance between ignoring one another and openly attending or observing one another as they pass in and out of one another's presence. What is communicated by this is the individual's confidence that others do not mean him harm, that he is not suspicious of their motives and is therefore not watching their moves apprehensively. The rule is, of course, routinely broken—people do stare over newspapers at others—but at the same time they acknowledge the existence of the rule by not staring *openly*. Similarly, bystanders normally extend civil inattention to persons engaged with one another. They acknowledge the existence of the engagement but quickly turn their attention away from it, so that they appear not to violate the "social space" of the engaged parties. It is not proper, for example, to openly eavesdrop on conversations between persons at an adjoining restaurant table.

A striking infringement of this rule has to do with the violation of engagement boundaries at the Short Grass swimming pool, a relatively small public recreation facility intended for the town's young people. The pool is frequented by a disproportionate number of girls on weekday mornings and afternoons (most boys being at work then). A wooden fence about five feet tall shields the bathers from the view of most passersby. But on one side the fence is lower, and I observed that a small group of Indian men would often stand there watching the bathers sun themselves. Their presence was not inconspicuous, since one of them could be heard from time to time offering a remark in Cree for the amusement of the others. Aside from using the edge of the pool farthest from the fence, the bathers did not acknowledge the Indians' presence: that is, they retreated and then extended the Indians "nonperson" status.[7]

Indians who stand on street corners, openly observing passersby, often violate the rule of civil inattention, as do those who sit in a cafe or pub studying the interaction of others. And it is usual to see Indians on the fringes of some White activity, silently watching children at a playground, men working, or people talking to one another. At public events, too, Indians remain outside activities, watching. For example, at the local stampede, Indians always collect at a spot a hundred yards from the arena, behind the chutes, from which they cannot see the animals or contestants emerge; but

[7] One can only guess at why Indians did not use the facility. Some reasons are, I think, lack of money and proper bathing dress. Moreover, Indians display great modesty regarding the body, more than would permit them to appear in bathing costumes. On the reserve, although men and women do swim together in a beaver pond, they stay fully clothed, removing only shoes and socks.

the slight elevation of their vantage point allows them to observe the stampede audience itself.

Of course, infractions of civil inattention can take widely varied forms. In Short Grass, one of the most frequent violations of both social distance between involved persons and the closure of engagements to bystanders occurs in Indians' attempts to penetrate these boundaries. For example, in a crowded pub on a weekend afternoon:

Pat Bowers, Loren McHugh, and another man were sitting at a table with one open chair. John Deersleep sauntered over to the table, grinning broadly. He stood for a few seconds, his presence unnoticed, then sat down. The three continued to disregard him, in spite of his efforts to establish verbal contact. . . . Finally, after two or three minutes, Loren turned and said, "What do you want?" John replied, "Oh, I was just gonna buy you a glass of beer." The third man said, "Yeah, and then you'll want us to buy you a dozen. We know those tricks." Again John was ignored. He turned his chair slightly away from the table, sat with hands in pockets gazing around the room for several minutes, and then returned to our table. "Them sonofabitches," he muttered to no one in particular.

Such rebuffs of Indians attempting encounters with Whites occur frequently, and are regarded by Whites as legitimate responses to the trespass of boundaries.

Putting Indians in Their Place

We have seen that Indians, in small ways and large, appear to Whites as irresponsible, untrustworthy, and childishly impulsive. The "trouble" regularly seen as caused by Indians is met by Whites with certain kinds of recurrently applied sanctions.

Aside from the fines and jail terms meted out to Indians for actual violations of the legal code, the most common technique is avoidance. Many Whites simply do not go to places where they expect to find bothersome Indians, such as the one Short Grass cafe most frequented by band members; in fact, some people drive nearly ten miles to a cafe where Indians are almost never present. In the summer a nearby provincial park offers a similar refuge. Other Whites avoid places like pubs altogether, as a middle-aged rancher explained: "I like to have a beer as much as anybody, but you just can't go in there any more without being bothered by them [Indians], wanting to sit with you and buttin' in. . . . If I want a beer, I just take some home, or go to somebody's house." This aversion was communicated to me by a number of persons, especially women, who would claim to enjoy visiting pubs in Cross Point and elsewhere but not in Short Grass.[8]

This avoidance can take subtler forms, as when Whites on the street avoid the gaze of Indians, refusing the eye contact that could be the opening of an unwanted engagement—especially since Indians cannot be trusted to extend civil inattention. Or Whites may cross a street to avoid an Indian approaching from the other direction, sometimes initiating an elaborate ballet. One quiet weekday morning,

A White (whom I could later see was Tom Roberts) walked south (in my direction) on the right-hand sidewalk. He was about two blocks away, and I saw Carl Russell walking toward him (north) on the same side of the street. Tom crossed the street diagonally, and Carl did the same. When they were about a block apart, Tom crossed again (at a sharper angle); so did Carl. When they were half a block apart, Tom again crossed, this time straight across, walking quickly into the savings and loan. Carl made no attempt to follow, stood for a minute watching Tom's withdrawal, and continued down the street. I could not see Tom's face, but I could see that he walked both with his head lowered and, after the second crossing, with increased determination, i.e., as if he had urgent business at the savings and loan.

Similar to this is a "nonperson" treatment like that employed at the Short Grass pool. This amounts to refusing to extend civil attention to Indians by acknowledging their presence. In Short Grass, it is the most common response to an Indian's infraction of the component of civil inattention that discourages people from openly staring at others. Thus Indians who sit in the town park near the street are not acknowledged by passersby, who will ordinarily "nod" to a White person resting there. Similarly Indians

[8] In the mid-60's, when a municipal vote was held to permit women in the pubs, the strongest reason given against the proposal was that Indian women would flock there and "cause trouble."

who hail a White on the street may not be responded to, the White
person hurrying off so that the Indian does not catch up with him.
Nonperson treatment can also include talking about someone as
though he were not there. At one point I heard an Indian agent
discuss with a rancher the possibility of the latter's grazing cattle
on the reserve; this took place in the presence of several Indians
(who had just approached), and the conversation was concluded
without the participants' having consulted the Indians about their
wishes, or even having acknowledged their presence.

To be treated as a nonperson is one way of not receiving civil
inattention from others. Another is to be openly observed by
others. For Whites to be the objects of Indian curiosity is an infraction of the rules by the Indian; but Indians may be stared
at as a matter of course, especially when they are "misbehaving."
To act improperly is to invite the attention of bystanders.

Scene in drugstore. It is a hot day (lower 90's, humid), and I am rooting
through the magazine stand. Through the drugstore window, the lady
clerk and two other White women customers can see Margaret Deersleep,
Ed Russell, another Indian girl, and several kids standing in front of the
hardware store across the street. The Indians cannot (or do not) see their
observers. Clerk says, "It's hot, ain't it?" One customer replies, "Yes, but
not too hot for Indians; look at 'em standing out there in the street, in
the sun." "Yes," the clerk agrees, "and those poor little children. You'd
think their parents would keep 'em out of the sun, or at least get 'em
some soda pop to cool 'em off a little." The second customer concurs,
"Yes, that's terrible."

During this, Margaret and the other girl begin an animated conversation, with much gesturing. It becomes more heated; the gestures become
more menacing and develop into a shouting match. Ed, holding back a
couple of steps from Margaret, does not look too comfortable. We in the
store, of course, can see but not hear what is happening. The clerk says,
"Look at that, right out in the street," and by this time all have dropped
their concerns to watch the show. First customer, laughing: "She really
looks mad, I wonder what it's all about." Second customer: "Who knows?
Probably over who's gonna buy the next bottle."

Margaret, accompanied by a small child, turns her back to the confrontation and starts off down the street. But she turns to deliver a parting shot, and the other girl runs toward her. The clerk says, amusedly,
"Oh, boy, it looks like we're gonna have a real fistfight now." They all

gaze intently out of the window, and we can see that a few passersby have also stopped on the street to watch. Again, Margaret turns and storms off, and her antagonist herself starts off in the opposite direction. The clerk says, "Well, I guess it's too hot even for *them* to have a go at each other."

A parallel situation was evident, and even more public, when I heard an announcer at the Short Grass stampede describe over the loudspeaker a bucking horse about to be ridden as "black as the inside of a squaw's moccasin."

Thus Indians, probably because they are counted upon to violate others' social space, are themselves open to unabashed scrutiny and comment, and even interference by Whites. This happens frequently in the pubs. On a slow weekday evening:

Charlie Russell was sitting with us, in a good mood and loquacious but not drunk. He had just been paid by Bill McIntosh for helping put up hay. After a while he moved to a nearby table to talk with two ranchers he knew. The conversation, though not loud, was audible at adjacent tables. They were talking about a new kind of plastic baling twine, and Charlie, though conceding its advantages, said, "Yes, but it tears up your goddam hands when you go to stack bales." [The bales are picked up and handled by this twine.] Sitting at the next table were two well-dressed men (in neckties), obviously strangers, who dropped their own conversation and began to listen to Charlie, who was in an expansive mood. The waiter had also been listening, and left the room. He called the police, complaining that Charlie was using "loud and foul language," and asked them to come. He then returned, went to Charlie's table and began to violently scold him. Charlie protested that he wasn't talking any worse than anyone else. A shouting match developed, and by this time all heads were turned, watching the exchange. Charlie stalked out of the place. [He was stopped outside and arrested, and spent the night in jail.]

To summarize, we have seen that social behavior in any context is governed by established rules of comportment, although these rules may be vague and not easily articulated by the actors. These rules, in turn, are implicated in organizing social intercourse, and are themselves shaped by more general value standards (self-control, industry, reliability, etc.). And whether the rules are observed or not, they directly give comment on the selves of persons present to one another. Of course, when the rules are repeatedly violated

THE PRESERVATION OF SELF

by a person or a category of persons, the selves expressed suffer. Such is the case with Short Grass Indians. In matters large or small, their performances fall short of White standards, and their situated selves are stigmatized. Moreover, this White judgment of Indians has been generalized across situations, so that Indians are seen as inherently profane persons who cannot be trusted to negotiate polite society. As a consequence, Indians are often greeted with open suspicion by Whites, and are denied the courtesies surrounding civil inattention. An Indian may find himself excluded from interaction he has tried to initiate, just as he may find himself approached by a White at will, as an "open" person.

A further point, though perhaps an obvious one: If one mentions all of this to Short Grass Whites (as I did repeatedly in the course of my fieldwork), one is told that the characteristic ways in which Indians are treated as profane are their own fault. Because they are rule-breakers, they cannot expect to receive ordinary social amenities. It is the Indian response to these circumstances that I wish to describe in the next three chapters.

So far, I have described Indian self-attributes from the White perspective, and have outlined the kinds of behavior that Short Grass Whites regard as confirming their image of Indian social selves. To Whites, the diverse attributes evidenced by Indian miscomportment denote a moral destitution. Ordinary interactional amenities are neither expected from Indians nor extended to them. This is not a trivial matter, since it incriminates Indians as profane persons. Respectable Whites protect themselves from these undesirables through numerous devices, as we saw in Chapter 5. But Short Grass Indians, in turn, have adopted a number of strategies to defend their assailed moral worth.

In general, persons who possess a seriously blemished identity find that it provokes others to treat them in a special way, as if they were contaminating. But the extent to which this is so depends partly on the visibility of the "stigma" and the possibility of concealing it. Thus we have the well-known phenomenon of "passing," in which a stigmatized person completely hides his failing and enters into normal interactions with normal people, but remains ever alert to the danger of being found out for what he is. Plastic surgery, a change of name, a manufactured past, a separation from those who know of one's stigma—these and many other techniques may be employed to pursue this double life. However, there are some profane persons whose stigma is always visible, and these people can only attempt to reduce the degree to which their failing obtrudes on their interactions with others. Their efforts are very similar to the techniques used in passing, but of necessity are only partially successful.

The partial strategy, called "covering" (Goffman, 1963b: 102), implies at least some acquiescence by the stigmatized to others' standards, and some recognition of the objectionable or discrediting nature of the stigma. Covering may also represent an assimilative orientation to the morally superior world, in the sense that the discredited person attempts to veil those self-attributes that discredit him and to win a measure of acceptance by "normals." Short Grass Indians, since they are physically identifiable as such, employ covering as one assimilative technique.[1] Attempts to pass are not made, those having failed in the past. (Before Indians were allowed to purchase liquor in western Canada, according to one Indian man, "A few guys tried to cross for White men and get into the bars, but they didn't make it. . . . You couldn't get in if you looked Indian.") I do not mean to suggest that Short Grass Indians have deliberately set out to become assimilated to White society. Rather, having perceived that there is something discreditable about themselves in White eyes, they attempt to play this something down, so that tension between themselves and Whites will be minimized. And they are surprisingly successful in this.

In previous chapters, it was indicated that many of the "old ways" remain—that much of Indian culture is intact, although its integrity is lost. This is especially true of religion, but is also the case with language, medicine, food habits, music, and recreation. Given all this, the extent to which Short Grass Whites are unaware of the band's Indianness is remarkable. Over and over, I was told that the Indians knew nothing about the old ways, that it was fruitless to seek such knowledge among them. One man said: "If you really want to know about Indians, go and look up some of the old-timers who were here when there were still *real*

---

[1] It is not the only one, of course; Indians do other things to win a place with Whites. The case of the Antelope brothers' attempts at self-support is a good example. Also, from time to time, most Indians give up drinking and other sorts of "antisocial" behavior. And some Indian parents, thinking of the future, are concerned that their children receive a formal education.

Indians around; they can tell you. Those guys up there don't know nothin' any more." Another claimed, "There's nothing special about them, they're just a bunch of drunks." The same man later expressed great surprise when informed of the extent to which the Cree culture was intact, exclaiming, "Why I never knew that that stuff still goes on up there."

This ignorance is the more curious when one considers the great fascination of local Whites with local and Western history. The Short Grass paper regularly runs stories and photos extolling the old days; and many families subscribe to magazines about the Old West, which include articles on Indian lore. The small town library contains volumes on the subject, and there is also a network of ranchers who circulate privately printed books about frontier history; one woman even persuaded a number of old-timers to write their memoirs for this purpose. Indians, being a necessary part of the traditional cowboy/frontier image, receive proportionate interest. Yet the Short Grass Whites, who could with little effort find "informants" close by, are unaware of this, and even deny that the band members know about, much less practice, "Indian" customs.

Indian Names

I mentioned earlier that on the reserve only Cree is spoken. In keeping with this, band members use only Indian names on the reserve, employing their English names exclusively for contact with Whites. In a sense, then, the White people of Short Grass for the most part do not know who Indians are. Until a generation ago—that is, until Indian women began to have their babies in the hospital—band members did not receive English names at all until late childhood, or until they needed them. A White informant reported, for the 1920's and '30's: "This is how it happened. Say old John would come around to mend fences in the spring, and camp here with his family. He'd have his wife and kids along with him, and them that was old enough to help, I'd begin to recognize. We'd be workin' and I'd say, 'What's that boy's name?' And old John would scratch his head and say, 'Well, let's

call him Charlie.' " In my experience, most Indian mothers today
do not decide on a name for a child until after it is born, and relatives who come to visit at the hospital are consulted. Even then,
these names do not seem to be taken very seriously. One young
mother who stopped by our house on the way home to show us her
new baby could not remember the child's name when asked, and
had to be reminded of it by a companion.

Indians did not acquire English names until they began regular
intercourse with Whites, who needed a way to identify them; and
there are some elderly women on the reserve who have no English
names at all, since their contact with Whites has been practically
nonexistent for most of their lives. Nowadays, Indian children
are named at the hospital at birth, so that their names may be
added to the band list and to their birth certificates. English names
appear on Indians' drivers' licenses, health insurance cards, and
all the other documents that form a part of their biographies in
the White world.

For the entire Short Grass band there are only five surnames
(though there are always a few temporary "visitors" from other reserves with their own names). Three of these—Antelope, Deersleep, and Bullrobe—are translations of the Indian names of heads
of households at the time the reserve was established nearly 60
years ago. The other two are of English origin (e.g., Russell), and
no one remembers how they happened to be assigned to Indian
families. In any case, the assignment of surnames was clearly neces-
sitated by bureaucratic record-keeping, to ensure that no person
who was not properly related to a band member would be included
on the band list. Obviously, since children do not inherit a "last
name" in the Cree system, Indian names alone would not identify
the "legitimate" offspring of a bona fide band member.

In recent years, perhaps because of exposure to TV and movies,
the English first names given to Indian babies have become relatively exotic—Priscilla, Delvina, or Bernard, for example. Among
older children and adults, however, the repertoire of first names is
rather limited. Well over half the band members share their name
with at least one other person, and some names have always been
very popular (there are six Charlies, five Marys, four Gordons, and

so on). There are even two cousins, of about the same age, both named Margaret Antelope. By contrast, no two people share the same Indian name.

All this sometimes gives rise to confusion. For example, a White person may discuss with an Indian the activities of another Indian for some minutes, only to discover that they have been referring to two different Charlies. Commonly, this is avoided by routinely using Indians' full names to identify them. Because there are so few surnames, there is also confusion over what to call married women: should Irene *née* Antelope, be called Irene Antelope, Irene Russell, or Mrs. Gordon Russell in order to distinguish her from Irene Antelope *née* Russell? Part of the problem lies in Whites' uncertainty about what constitutes Indian marriage, that is, at what point a couple who are living together may be considered husband and wife. The problem does not exist in Cree-speaking contexts, since a woman does not change her name at marriage. Finally, in Short Grass, to know that Carl Russell is an Indian one must know that Russell is an "Indian" name.

On the reserve, an entirely different system of naming prevails and all band members have received an Indian name (*wihuwin*) by the age of three or four. Indians further distinguish between two such names: uʰ*keče wihuwin* (or *tapwe wihuwin*), a person's "real" (or "good") name; and *kuntia wihuwin*, a nickname ("nonsense name"). The two kinds of names are acquired by quite different procedures.

As in English, the real names of Cree identify particular individuals and locate them uniquely. But they do more than this. By their meaning, Indian names also indicate the specific guardian spirit under whose protection a person exists. To receive a name is thus to establish a personal relationship between the individual and one of the indefinite number of spirits in the Cree pantheon. Persons who are named Očo (fly), Wakayuš (bear), or Kisikawasis (day child), for instance, have specific spirits as their respective protectors. This is no trivial matter: one relies on one's guardian for both good fortune and good health; and this relationship with the supernatural profoundly affects an Indian's entire life. A namesake makes periodic gifts to his guardian, though there is no prescribed schedule for doing so. Usually, this involves hanging a yard or two of brightly colored cloth in a bush; sweet grass may be burned at the same time, and tobacco and prayers may be offered. The expected offering is greater during a crisis, such as an illness, or before the start of a difficult undertaking. Certain ritual occasions, such as the Sun Dance (more properly, Thirsting Dance), are also appropriate times to celebrate the sacred relationship. Many band members tell of times, especially during an illness, when they were visited by their guardians, who spoke to them and gave instructions to make some specific sacrifice.[2]

A name is truly a sacred thing. It links one to a source of supernatural power and, indirectly, to good fortune. A name signifies a dependency relationship between an Indian and the supernatural that profoundly affects the person's entire life. The warrant to give names at Short Grass, as with other ritual and ceremonial matters, is possessed by only a few. There are people who are empowered to conduct giveaway dances or to cure certain illnesses, for example; and there is one man who may "put up" a Sun Dance and is also the person most sought after as a namegiver (though one other man is allowed to give names). This holy man, in his sixties, is clearly respected by all reserve members, and is cared for by various households for a month or so in turn. He acquired his powers in the course of a vision quest at the age of about 15. On the fourth day of fasting, alone and naked on the prairie, he was visited by the Thunder Spirit and taken to the spirit world. Received there by a number of deities, he was told that henceforth he had the power to cure illness, to arrange certain ceremonies, including the Sun Dance, and to bestow names. The spirits also gave him a new name—Piyesikani[h] Tapwe, which he translates Thunder Good-talker—to signify his ability to commune easily with the spirits. He also retained his original name, Kasukapisut (Noise of Swift Lightning). After returning to the everyday world, he apprenticed himself to several old men who knew the way to

---

[2] A spirit helper may also make its presence known without giving verbal messages. For example, many Cree have names referring to one of the various manifestations of thunder (e.g., Kape[h] Tewituk, "thunder roaring") that can be heard from time to time. Guardian spirits also appear in dreams.

put up a Sun Dance and instructed him in the songs, prayers, and procedures involved.

Normally, Indian children are given their names at any age from about two to four. Until then, they are under the generalized protection of the Great Spirit, Keʰče Manitu, and are called by a kin term or endearment, or, less commonly, by their English name. Having decided to seek a name for his child, the father will approach the holy man, who prays for a revelation from his guardian. He may learn the child's name either in a dream or during a visit to the spirit world. When this has happened, he informs the parents, who prepare a small "baptism" for the child.

The father presents the namegiver with offerings for the spirits (usually cloth and tobacco), as well as a personal gift of tobacco and a small amount of money. The namer then prays to Keʰče Manitu, to the spirit that revealed the child's name, and to the child's new spirit helper, all of whom are asked to guard the child's health and good fortune. The namer then takes the child in his arms, pronounces its name, and blows four times on the nape of its neck, making the sound *hu!*[3] This is intended to infuse the child's soul with the power of the spirit protector indicated by its name. At this time the namer may briefly instruct the parents about the child's guardian, telling them, for example, the various ways in which the spirit may manifest itself. The ceremony proper concludes with the passing of the child to each of those present, who, in turn, pronounce his name and offer brief prayers for his welfare. The cloth offerings are placed on bushes at a later time. Should the parents be so inclined and have the financial resources, they will give a feast; it is up to them whether or not the occasion is made a social one (for example, in the summer of 1971 a child was named when there were few persons present on the reserve, and no meal was served).

A special relationship exists between a person and his namer through their lives. They use the reciprocal term *nikwene*, which Piyesikaniʰ Tapwe translates as "person the same as me" or "per-

---

[3] In Cree belief, the soul, or life force (*aʰčak*), resides in the nape of the neck; it enters the body at birth, departs at death or during sleep, and mediates all contact with the spirits.

son of the same body as mine." In later years, it is the person's namer who will be called on to help at times of sickness and on other occasions where supernatural aid is needed.

Most Short Grass band members have nicknames in addition to their sacred names. Some of these are nonsense words—a string of syllables with no lexical meaning at all. One man, for instance, is called Doman, just as in English a person might be called Bobo. Indians do not usually recall just how most such names were acquired, though in one case a woman was called by a nonsense name she had invented for herself as a small child. Unlike real names, nicknames may change during a person's lifetime. Frequently these temporary epithets refer to some physical characteristic of the named—e.g., such as Nahawis (Slim) or Kačakos (Shorty). When these are used, however, they are terms of affection, not ridicule.[4] Other people are known by terms such as Napesis (Boy) or Kesyineu (Old Man). Still another man is known as Gamistet, a corruption of his real name coined by his little daughter.

Nicknames, in addition to offering a way to express affection, also figure into the etiquette of name usage. In the old days it was considered improper to ask another Indian his name directly, or to use it in his presence.[5] The reason given for this is that a person's spirit helper, usually a source of good, can also cause misfortune or ignore prayers if it is insulted; and the casual use of a person's name, which is also the spirit's, is just such an affront. Probably the uttering of a person's name was considered an invasion of privacy, though we have no direct evidence of this.

In any case, it was formerly correct to employ a nickname or kinship term in place of a real name, and this usage is largely still

[4] It sometimes happens that children will use names as insults. I was once present when a six-year-old girl came running into her house in tears and cried to her mother that the other children were calling her "fish lips." She was taunted with this for several days before it was dropped. I know of one case of a man from another reserve who lived for several years with his Short Grass wife on the reserve. He did not speak Cree well, was generally unpopular, and was labeled Munias (White Man). This was usually used behind his back, and only thrown at him when people were drinking.

[5] Amelia Paget (1909: 107–10) says that although everyone in a community might know a person's name, it was never used, especially by near relatives.

in force on the Short Grass reserve, especially among older people. In such a small community, most people can trace some kin relationship to almost anyone in the group, and thus can use the appropriate term. In cases where no relationship exists, a term may be used figuratively. Two men may call one another *nistau* (brother-in-law). An elderly man may call a younger one *nosisim* (grandchild). Or a man may call a woman *ničimus* (female cross-cousin). Since cross-cousins are marriageable among the Cree, *ničimus* is sometimes used in jest to mean "sweetheart" (the reciprocal is *nitim*, male cross-cousin). Occasionally, a person's English name may be used. Thus it is possible to refer to or address any other band member without the person's real name. Older people seem to follow this rule more consistently; and we did several times hear younger persons use another's real name in his presence.

The taboo against asking a person his name directly is also still active at Short Grass. Before I knew this, whenever I asked someone for his or her name, or their child's name, I was told politely to ask someone else, though in no case did anyone deny having a name. (It is not considered impolite to ask some third party the name of a person not present.) Usually, I was directed to Piyesi-kani[h] Tapwe, who had named so many of the band members. I also asked various informants about the proper procedure to follow when two strangers must introduce themselves to one another. The consensus was that one begins by asking where the stranger is from and then trying to see if some kinship relation exists between them. One might also ask for a nickname, but would wait to ask a third person for the stranger's real name.

A final striking aspect of the use of names by band members is the absolute segregation observed. English is never spoken on the reserve, except when a non-Cree speaker is present; and not once did I hear an English name used in a flow of conversational Cree.[6]

---

[6] The kin terms I have given here were elicited in formal interviews, and names were learned in the course of less formal conversations. Although my wife and I did spend time working with informants on Cree grammar, I myself never progressed beyond being able to ask simple questions or follow the main points of a conversation. (My wife, however, became more fluent.)

In the same way, when Indians talked English, I never heard any Indian real names or nicknames.

The point of all of this is that, in keeping their real names from Whites, Indians are concealing a significant aspect of their identities—part of the core of their Indianness. In the town of Short Grass, of course, Whites who have little contact with Indians do not know any Indian by name; but even those who do know many Indians personally are seldom aware of anything but the Indians' English names. Or they may know only family names—e.g., "That's an Antelope girl." All of these Whites are ignorant of the fact that Indians have other, "real" names, and know nothing of the naming practices and etiquette prevailing on the reserve. One rancher, born in Short Grass, has employed Indian men for years, as did his father before him, and some of them have lived for extended periods on his property. But when I mentioned to him that a man who had been working for him for three years possessed an Indian name, the rancher was completely astonished: "I thought all those things died out years ago!"

Probably no more than a few dozen Whites have even a vague awareness of Indian names. Most of these are people who lived near the reserve as children and had regular contact with the Indians. The great majority, however, do not know any particular Indian by his or her real name. I met only four men who knew any Indian names, and two of these spoke some Cree. They were adults, in their fifties, who had played with Indians as children, and they knew the names of some of their former playmates, though not those of any Indians from later generations. For example, one rancher knew Margaret Deersleep's name (Skakits, "White Feather"), but not the names of any of her children or grandchildren. And even such knowledge as exists is often misinterpreted. Once, in a discussion involving a local rancher, the conversation turned to a chief, long dead, whom the rancher remembered from his childhood as "Bearskin." My wife asked for the Cree word and, in analyzing the compound, found that the name translated "one who has bare skin." At this, the rancher burst into laughter, say-

ing, "Why, I've lived here over forty years, and I always thought
that meant a man who wore a *bear*skin on his back."

What all of this means, I maintain, is that no White person (with
the four exceptions mentioned above) can identify any Indian in
the same way an Indian identifies himself. I use identify both in
the narrow sense of labeling a person as a unique biographical
individual and also in the broader sense of apprehending the "Indian" or Cree part of the individual's identity. Quite literally,
White members of the Short Grass community do not fully know
who their Indian neighbors are. And it is not just a case of Whites
not seeking such knowledge. Almost without exception, every
White with whom I discussed these matters expressed great interest and curiosity about Indian practices. Rather, Indians conceal
their real names from Whites. I asked many Indians why this was
done, and was told, "They couldn't pronounce them right," or
"They wouldn't understand." When pressed, however, nearly
every informant indicated that he would be "embarrassed," or
that he feared ridicule. This does happen: one Indian whose real
name of Piwapiskw'w'sis (Iron Child) was learned by a White is
referred to by that man as "Piss-Piss."

Indian Lore

Whites' ignorance of Indian names and naming reflects more
than simply Cree etiquette. It is part of a general unwillingness
on the part of Indians to reveal cultural differences that would
call attention to their Indianness, which they know is disparaged
by Whites and hinders interaction. Numerous practices that are
widespread on the reserve are nevertheless denied by Indians to
Whites. For example, I heard one White ask an Indian the purpose of the small bits of cloth hung here and there in bushes,
which the latter claimed not to know (some older Whites still
remember that these are offerings to spirits). Private religious
ritual, in particular, is not acknowledged even to those Whites
who ask about it, including Indian agents. For example, the rancher Frank Pope complained that he could never "pry" anything

about such matters out of his protégé Tony Dumont during their
long evening conversations (see Chapter 5). This is perfectly natural, considering Frank's intent to persuade Tony to reject the
Indian world for the White one.

Tony would just dummy up when I asked him anything about the reserve, like about "doctoring." He'd say, "I don't know," or "They don't
do that any more." He wouldn't tell me anything, even though we were
good friends and did talk about serious things.... They're absolutely
no different from the rest of us. Oh, in the old days they used to have
their own little culture all to themselves. But that's all gone. Now they're
no different than Whites.... They're drunks, that's how they're different.

Indians deny that such traditional crafts as leatherwork and
beadwork are done, though at least a dozen women on the reserve
still engage in them. Whites who come to the reserve and offer
generous sums for deerskin gloves or beaded belts have been turned
down with the explanation that these are lost arts.[7] One Indian
girl, asked about this refusal, said, "I guess they want to be more
like White folks." I then asked if she meant that people actually
did not do such work, or instead that they won't admit to Whites
that they do. "Well, yes," she replied, "I guess that's what they're
thinking; they don't want anybody to know."

Another instance of concealment concerned a Catholic priest
who at one point took a desultory interest in the band. He had
apparently received instructions to broaden his ecumenical activities and, along with a nun, visited the reserve several times. He
took an (inaccurate) census, and attempted to engage the Indians
in theological discussion, with little success. At one point, he asked
to be shown the Indian burial grounds and to be told something of
mortuary practices. As he explained it to me,

Old John took me to a place not far from the lower camp and showed me
a spot on the prairie. I couldn't see anything special about it, so I asked
him why we couldn't see any graves. You have to understand the Indian

---

[7] One White rancher was able to secure some gloves, but it is interesting to
note that he was a man with a relatively intimate knowledge of Indian "ways"
and was not unappreciative of them. As a child, he had lived near the reserve
and had had Indian playmates.

way, you see, the way it was explained. When they bury someone they put 'em in a hole and smooth it over carefully so that you can never tell where they're buried. They believe that the body is taken over by the Great Mother Earth and should disappear into it, I figured out. That's why you can never find the graves. Of course, I told old John that it would be better if they put up some sort of marker, anything, just so the person could be remembered, and family could visit if they wanted. And also, if anyone could see it was a grave, then it wouldn't be disturbed accidentally. But he didn't seem to understand.

I listened to the man's further revelation of "Indian burial practices," and it was quickly evident that he had, in fact, not been taken to the place where bodies are interred. This is in the hills, in a plot that is carefully fenced in, and individual graves, though unmarked, are clearly identifiable. The priest, however, had been shown some vacant spot on the prairie. He had been had.

I do not wish to enumerate all the items of Indian culture unknown to Whites, even if it were possible to do so exhaustively. Some of these, in fact, such as the practice of distinguishing cross-cousins from parallel cousins (the former being marriageable), would be difficult for Whites to comprehend. What is clear, however, is that White ignorance of Indian customs is extensive, and that the same customs are (among other things) a source of embarrassment or "shyness" in Indians. An Indian woman, talking with my wife about child-rearing, explained how to construct a type of sling for carrying a baby on the back, adding that it was a very convenient arrangement. But, she said, she would never use this in town because she was afraid that she would "look funny" and people would stare.

It appears that Indians are especially reluctant to acknowledge to Whites anything that might be seen as quaint superstition. At the beginning of our fieldwork we elicited many stories from the old days concerning miraculous events and the appearance of spirits or supernatural beings. These tales were always begun, ended, and punctuated with "this is a true story" (*ékusi itéu*). One informant added that of course such things did not happen much any more, since the spirits had retreated after the coming of the Whites. But, as we discovered after a time, the spirit world—both evil and benevolent—is still quite active. Wondrous things still happen, although the spirits make themselves known only to Indians and not to Whites. When he knew us well, one informant reported hearing spirits talking to him, receiving visitations from the Thunderbird, and having scrapes with ghosts. And, of course, no Indian doubts the efficacy of love medicine or bad medicine.

In general, the supernatural seems to be the most sensitive area of Cree culture, and that which Indians are most "secretive" about. They disapprove of Christianity, arguing that it is not for Indians: "We got our own better religion." And Indian jokes like the following are common.

Two Indians went hunting, with no luck. They were far from camp when night came. They were lost. They wandered around for a long time, but could not find their way home. They tried everything. Finally one said, "Maybe I'll try praying to the White God." So he got down on his knees and said "God, if you show us the way home, when we get there I'll give you that new colt I got."

The second Indian poked his friend in the side and said, "What are you saying? You don't have a colt!"

"Shush," the first whispered, "He'll hear you."

Indians who have some knowledge of Christianity accuse Whites of hypocrisy, pointing out that they constantly break their own rules against working on the Sabbath and fail to show Christian charity and generosity.[8]

Although Indians consider their religion superior to that of Whites, they are unwilling to speak about it to Whites, even when questioned directly. In part, this seems to result from what they perceive as the Whites' defamatory attitude. For example, the Sun Dance lodge, a round structure of center post and radiating poles, is always left standing after the ceremony and allowed to crumble with time; meanwhile, it is considered a sacred object. There are about a dozen old lodges on the reserve, in various stages of deterioration, and a neighboring White rancher periodically offers to purchase them for use in making fenceposts. The Indians to

[8] With the exception of several children, unaccountably listed as Roman Catholic, all band members are described on the list as of aboriginal religion.

whom he makes this offer invariably refuse it without explanation. They regard his proposals as an affront; he, in turn, regards their refusal as inexplicable stubbornness. In another case, the only White visitor to the 1967 Sun Dance (other than myself) was a local businessman, who came out of curiosity and asked if he could photograph the ceremony. He was not allowed to take any pictures inside the lodge, and left after taking a few of the people outside.

The isolation of the reserve effectively blocks White observation of the band's activities. And the Indians' own disinclination to divulge information about themselves is part of a generalized reticence toward Whites. They assume a blank look when questioned about reserve affairs, at most muttering, "I don't know." One White man complained that Indians tell "barefaced" lies. I heard him question an Indian about a scuffle that the White claimed to have witnessed near the reserve, in which one man had been knocked unconscious. He pressed for details of the incident, but the Indian claimed to know nothing. "Goddammit!" the White said, "Don't tell me that. You were there when it happened, I *saw* you." But his questions were never answered.

In interactions with Whites, Indians are never permitted to "forget they are Indians," but are constantly reminded of what they are by the special treatment they receive. The attention called to their status may not be verbally expressed, but it is nevertheless pervasive. Knowing that Whites define Indianness as morally inferior, they take the measures needed to "cover" undesirable communications about things Indian. One consequence of this is that the tension between themselves and Whites is often submerged beneath the surface of their encounters.

Noble Savage, Ignoble Indian

We can use the term "covering" to describe the process of Indians' concealing their identities, then, but only with several qualifications. First, White views are more complex than a simple equation of "Indian" with "bad"; for, as we have seen, it is contemporary Indians who are condemned, not Indians of the past. Although the history of Short Grass is only three generations old,

Whites regard the town's early days with nostalgia, as a romantic period when men faced hardship in a challenging environment. And the qualities demanded of the men who prevailed—determination and strength, thrift and ingenuity—are still admired. Newspaper obituaries of Short Grass old-timers are more than simple death notices. Usually, they are more like short biographies, recounting the deceased's early hardships and extolling his courage, honesty, and resoluteness.

Indians are necessarily part of this nostalgia, and the names of famous chiefs like Poundmaker, Piapot, and Sitting Bull are often mentioned. Since western Canada never experienced the bloody Indian wars that took place south of the border, these reminiscences do not contain the bitterness of remembered massacres or battles. Indians are portrayed as brave but mysterious hunters of the buffalo, as great horsemen, and as persons of considerable dignity. Ranchers whose land has never been plowed have even located and protected the sites of ancient Indian camping grounds where circles of stones used to hold down the sides of tepees still remain. The paintings of C. W. Russell, who represented Indians romantically and with sympathy, are much admired in Short Grass, and prints of them are in great demand. When Russell's famous "Invocation to the Sun," depicting a solitary mounted Indian at prayer, was reproduced on a calendar put out by a garage in town, the supply was quickly exhausted, and the calendars were prominently hung in many town and rural homes.

It is probably true that Indian-White relations were less strained in the old days. In any event, the pioneer image—and Short Grass Whites like to think they are made of the same stuff—necessarily requires the presence of feathered and painted noble savages. The image of the frontiersman, adventuresome and dauntless, is drawn in a hostile environment that includes potentially dangerous red men of exotic culture. Conflict, when it did occur, at least consisted of "honest fights" (although, as old-timers recollect, danger from Indians in the region was usually more imagined than real). The historical accuracy of these views is beside the point. What is important is that Whites see things this way and regard themselves as direct inheritors of the old traditions. The manly qualities valued on the Frontier are still expected and rewarded at present.

It is at this point that Short Grass Indians come in for another sort of disapproval: they are regarded as culturally impoverished and degenerate, as having failed to maintain their traditions and preserve the colorfulness they once possessed. Contemporary practices reflect this. At stampede time and at other community festivities, Whites customarily dress up in old-fashioned clothes and parade in old buggies or buckboards; many men let their beards grow for the occasion. Indians attend these events primarily as spectators. They are occasionally asked to "powwow"—to dress up in Indian clothes and dance. But this happens with decreasing frequency, since Whites complain that the costumes are poorly made and unauthentic, and that Indians must be paid to perform. As one man said: "Hell, we celebrate 'cause it's fun, but them buggers got to be *paid* to put on a half-assed show."

Indians' covering, then, is based on a misunderstanding of the dual connotation the word Indian has for Whites. They hide their "realness," to the displeasure of Whites, displaying instead what appears to Whites as shiftlessness, irresponsibility, and dissipation. Here we encounter a major contradiction in White opinion. The Indians' authenticity is denigrated, and they are thought to have lost touch with their traditions. Even Whites who recognize that some things remain regard these as "fake." For example, some Whites who knew of the Sun Dance spoke of its practice by the Short Grass band as if it were a hollow reproduction of the "real thing," even though they had never seen it.[9] But at the same time while criticizing Indians for failing to live up to their old traditions (or at least to the White conception of these), Whites also criticize Indians for not being "White" enough. The major Indian failing cited in this regard is that of self-sufficiency, the contention being that before and during the frontier period Indians supported themselves.

Essentially, the Short Grass Whites assert their own moral su-

---

[9] This view is not restricted to Short Grass. I heard White tourists at a large, extensive Sun Dance in the U.S. proclaim to one another their disappointment at the "show," exclaiming, "Why, they're dressed just like cowboys. There's nothin' to this at all."

periority, and explain their relative affluence, by a simple line of reasoning: Indians are poor because they are shiftless; and they are shiftless because they have given up old customs but not adopted new ones (that is, White ones). This was clearly illustrated in the remarks of a woman shopkeeper who felt that something "needed to be done" about the Indians. "They could get jobs easy if they'd show some responsibility, if you could count on them to be steady. They don't have to stop being Indians, just work up some self-respect." When she was reminded that attendance at Sun Dances required some summer nomadism, the woman concluded emphatically, "Well, they'll just have to give up the Sun Dance, that's all."

An additional qualification to the conclusion that Short Grass Indians "cover" their Indianness may be noted. Conduct that many Whites regard as reprehensible may in fact be seen as reflecting some continuity between past and present: that is, it may be an Indian behavior pattern of long standing. Indians do not share the White ideas that work is an end in itself, that success can be measured by the accumulation of material goods, or that punctuality is a virtue (in fact, Indians jokingly distinguish between "Indian time" and "White time"). The ethnographic literature suggests that standards opposed to these were dominant precontact values among the Cree, and not simply responses to White contact (see, for example, Jefferson, 1929: 63). But Short Grass Whites, ignorant of traditional Cree custom, do not even consider this possibility. In condemning Indians for breaking with their past, then, Whites are imposing both their own ideas of the "noble" redman and their own interpretation of the values communicated by present-day Indian conduct. What they seem to demand is a Cree who meets all the standards by which they judge "colorful" Indians and at the same time has all the qualities they value most in Whites.

Drunken Indians

I have suggested that what Indians conceal from Whites is based on a misunderstanding. But this raises a second question. Given that Indians conceal many aspects of their traditional culture, why do they not also conceal other sorts of behavior that Whites disapprove of? Why does an Indian hide his name, his religion, and so on, in the interest of covering his Indianness but at the same time be seen staggering out of a pub in the stereotyped role of a drunken Indian? There are only two (elderly) men on the Short Grass reserve who do not drink. All the remaining men, and many women, have been to court for various liquor violations, with their names duly announced in the police court column of the newspaper. Now, drinking is one of the faults that Whites most frequently single out in censuring Indians, and every Indian is aware of this. Indeed, it is expressed to them by Whites in numerous contexts—sometimes contemptuously and sometimes sympathetically, in subtle and not so subtle ways. If the Indians' goal was assimilation through covering one would expect them to either moderate or conceal their use of alcohol.

The reasons for this contradictory behavior are complex, but one factor that contributes to the heavy drinking is probably mutual reinforcement. Indians who go on the wagon are inevitably drawn back to drinking by other band members, whom they can not, after all, avoid. Another factor (to be discussed in Chapter 8) is that as ritually profane persons Indians have little to lose when they appear drunk in a public place. For whatever reasons Indians drink, though, I think that one important element in their doing so openly is that they do not identify their behavior as specifically and exclusively Indian. Although Whites see Indians as a special group of congenital alcoholics, Indians themselves know that their behavior is little different from that of many White men. Indians are quick to cite the fact that on Saturday nights the Short Grass pubs are filled with drunken, boisterous cowboys, some of whom seek Indian company to continue drinking on the reserve or at the nuisance grounds after closing time. And there are always as many or more Whites mentioned in the police court column. Indians therefore see drinking as a sort of behavior learned from Whites, and even encouraged by some of them; indeed, until drinking rights were recently granted Indians had to rely on illegal White assistance to secure alcohol. In sum, Indians do not see their own behavior with regard to drinking as setting them apart from Whites. What they do cover is that which they regard as most Indian—names, religious beliefs, and so on.

The drinking problem illuminates still another aspect of Indian orientation to the White world. Covering is a strategy that seems to work for many categories of stigmatized individuals, such as the handicapped or the members of minority ethnic groups. And the closer it approaches "passing" the more successful it is, since it allows an increased sacredness of self and brings the rewards of unstrained interaction with the nonstigmatized. For many categories of profane persons, however, the complications that confront Short Grass Indians do not arise. Usually, stigmatized persons are aware of the standards that define their failing, and in fact share the cultural identity values that define them as stigmatized. But in Short Grass there are, in effect, two different sets of identity values, as we have seen in the case of drinking behavior.

Another way of approaching the question is to look at what we mean by guilt.[10] Guilt, as Lynd suggests (1958: 208), "involves transgression of a specific code." When the code is unknown, one can be guilty unawares—which in our prevailing Western code makes no difference, since one is still guilty. Now, Indians do not express feelings of guilt about drinking, nor do they normally hold one another responsible for their actions while intoxicated. It happened over and over again during my stay that some Indian became aggressive or even violent while drunk, damaged his or someone else's car or truck, or was unfaithful to a spouse. "He was drinking" was considered an adequate explanation of such behavior, and the matter was dropped. A man who had been menacingly belligerent to family and friends the night before would be treated no differently than anyone else the following day. There would be no remonstrations, and if anything was said it was in a joking tone. A term in jail—for Indians, nearly always associated with drinking—is likewise no stigma on the reserve, and is part of

[10] Shame, of course, is another problem altogether. For a discussion of the contrast between the two, see Lynd, 1958: 204–10; see also Piers and Singer, 1953.

the experience of almost every adult male and of many females. It is not something to be carefully concealed, and in casual conversation band members will speak of jail without reticence, bitterness, or any sign of a sense of guilt.

Feeling guilty for transgressing a moral rule is not the same as being guilty. One feels guilty when one's action is felt as a blemish on the inner self, when one has violated standards that are accepted as part of one's identity and are used to evaluate one's own moral worth. Obviously, Indians do not experience the guilt that Whites associate with their own drinking and readily use to evaluate Indians' drinking. There is one very revealing exception to this pattern. During the Sun Dance liquor is forbidden, and no one present in the circle of tents around the sacred lodge may possess or consume it. This rule is observed and enforced by the majority of the band; and the few who break it are scolded, a sanction apparently strong enough to dissuade infractions by most of the community. This is the sole occasion on which drinking appears to be a source of felt guilt on the reserve. When I asked why alcohol was forbidden at this time and at no other, an Indian man replied positively: "Because the Sun Dance is an Indian thing and drinking is a White thing."

To recapitulate what I have tried to convey in this chapter, Short Grass Indians know very well that they are outcasts, that Whites regard them as profane persons, and that the category Indian is equated with moral decrepitude. In the interest of bettering their moral status, then, they attempt to cover from Whites the things they themselves feel to be characteristically and essentially Indian, either misconstruing or ignoring White attitudes toward their other behavior. But as we shall see, their efforts have brought them very little in the way of moral elevation.

ANOTHER WAY Indians deal with their understanding of the prevailing White attitude toward them is to withdraw, seeking a measure of self-regard within the Indian community. It is an understandable tactic. As Cooley has observed (1964: 250): "Mortification, resentment, jealousy, the fear of disgrace and failure . . . are exhausting passions; and it is after a severe experience of them that retirement seems most healing and desirable." The withdrawal of Indians, as we shall see, involves a kind of seclusion, and a substitution of what they see as uniquely Indian values for repudiated White ones. This tactic is analytically distinct from covering in that covering involves some acknowledgment of White values: Indian ways are covered not out of mere secretiveness but because of their potential for embarrassment. In the process I describe in this chapter, what is Indian is held up as preferable to what is White, at least among band members. And one of the most important Indian values in this regard is that of sharing and reciprocal generosity. I shall raise some questions about what may be seen as inconsistencies in Indian thought and behavior, and suggest an interpretation that renders these understandable in their interactional context.

In Short Grass, Indians place great positive regard on sharing one's resources with others, and on doing so generously. Conversely, they are strongly critical of people they consider stingy or greedy. Nonetheless, there are occasions when the behavior required by this standard appears to be onerous to Indians, that is, when they would obviously prefer not to share resources of various kinds. It quite often happens, in fact, that Short Grass Indians employ elaborate techniques of evasion and secrecy in order to avoid sharing. Why, then, is the positive value of sharing maintained even when people will go to considerable lengths in order to avoid having to honor it? What is it that perpetuates the value? Note that this question is the reverse of asking why Indians sometimes resent having to share, or why they so often violate a rule about which they are so articulate. I will deal here mostly with the first problem—why the value persists despite its frequent breach—since the answer has important implications not only for interaction within the Indian community but also for relations between Indians and Whites. How Indians discover and maintain a morally defensible definition or image of self is the major concern of this study. Obviously, a worthy self cannot be maintained in an interactional vacuum, but must be publicly validated by others; and among the Cree, sharing and generosity are deeply involved in this process.

Plains Philanthropists

In their heyday the Plains Cree were bison hunters, organized into a number of bands that for much of the year were divided into smaller nomadic groups. When an entire band assembled, notably at the time of the Sun Dance, matters were directed by a band chief. The chief's authority was not formally constituted, however, and he was essentially a redistributor of wealth in the form of horses, guns, and other valuables. As Jefferson observes (1929: 67): "Running the buffalo was the work of the young men, while the old accumulated the equipment. With two or three buffalo-runners and a couple of rifles, one could be sure of plenty to eat, and numerous adherents. Hence, a chief." It was only through generosity with the items needed for hunting that a man could validate claims to leadership; and such generosity provided most of the social integration for these roving bands. Indeed, the Cree word for chief, *okimau*, is a derivation of the verb meaning "to give away."

With the expansion of the fur trade, Indians were able to obtain European goods from the Hudson's Bay Company (and later from American firms), for which they bartered furs and pemmican. Such transactions were usually made through the "chief," who bargained for the band as a whole. Because of this, White traders could virtually select chiefs: they had merely to pass over an uncooperative man and deal with someone more manageable, who then became able to display the generosity demanded of a chief. To Whites, the transactions were a strictly economic exchange of furs for guns and powder; but to Indians they were infused with considerable ritual significance, and it appears that this aspect of the matter was never fully grasped by Whites. One trader, in his memoirs, complained about the unbusinesslike disposition of Indians:

Now, an Indian was never satisfied with a trade which was a fair and exact exchange, at the fixed prices of the time, until he had received "something for nothing" at the top of the transaction. It did not matter if a trader raised the prices of furs and lowered the prices of goods to him on the distinct understanding that no present was to be expected or given, the Indian always expected that "something for nothing" so dear to all man- and womankind, at the end of the barter. (Cowie, 1911: 195)

Indians came to be known not as "hard bargainers" in the White sense but rather as importunate and demanding. Chiefs, in particular, wanted fancy scarlet coats, top hats, and other such gewgaws as insignia of their relationship with the White traders. To the Indians—the "children" of the Queen and her agents—the inequality of the exchange when a gift was thrown in was symbolic of the traders' superiority in wealth and power, just as the same relation was expressed in unequal exchanges between a chief and his followers. Loyalty and submission were extended to those who could be counted upon to be generous with material goods.

What's Mine Is Yours (and Vice Versa)

Today, of course, there is no chief as such in the Short Grass band, and his position as benefactor has been taken over by the

Indian agent. Resources are fairly evenly distributed among the band, so that no single person is able to assume a position of importance by unusual generosity, as was possible in the old days. But sharing and generosity are still valued as personal qualities, and a person who has money, food, or any other resource is expected to unhesitatingly and ungrudgingly distribute it to others. One case from my field notes illustrates the general attitude:

Sam Timber returned to the reserve today, after an absence of almost two weeks. He's been working for a rancher near Maplewood [about 40 miles distant], and seems to have made it back with most of his pay. He was driven up by McLane [a townsman who runs an irregular "taxi" service]. Sam was dressed in new Levis, shirt, and belt. He got out at Charlie Antelope's house (where he had been staying), and carried in a box containing two gallons of wine, a carton of cigarettes, candy and soda for the kids, and some beef. Sam said expansively to the dozen or so people who are always near Charlie's place, "Come on inside, have a drink. . . . There's plenty for everybody." This was about one in the afternoon. A small crowd gathered, singing began, and there was much merriment. Sam presided over the occasion, encouraging everyone to drink up and share his presents. . . . About 6:30 the wine was gone, but singing continued until about 7:30. Then Sam, still in an expansive mood, along with three of the Antelope boys and four or five girls . . . took off for town in Charlie's truck.

When Sam returned to the reserve next day, all his money was gone; but he showed no apparent regret at this, seeming as cheerful as the day before.

Such "distribution" of resources is a common event on the reserve, and anyone present is always included. On a less conspicuous scale, anyone present when a meal is served in an Indian house is served with the rest without being asked if he wants to eat. Similarly, anyone heading into town will be hailed by others who also want to go, so that most such trips are made by as many as can squeeze into the vehicle. On the reserve it is not considered improper, as it is among Whites, to ask for someone's last cigarette; to refuse such a request, however, is frowned upon.

The importance of giving is also expressed in ritual and ceremonial. In the winter "giveaway dances" are held, at which everyone contributes to a preliminary feast. This is followed by singing, during which individuals, in turn, dance around the room and distribute pieces of clothing, watches, knives, or anything else that can be considered a "present." One object of this behavior is to give away more than one receives, so as to demonstrate one's unconcern for material things. And I have known men who gave particularly generous gifts to another man they did not like in order to humiliate him and demonstrate their own superiority. The giveaway ceremony today appears to be a more secular affair than in the old days (see Mandelbaum, 1940: 275–76), when it was directed to the spirit world; and it is essentially an occasion for conviviality and socializing.

The Sun Dance, too, contains elements of this sharing ideology. It is basically a reciprocal exchange with the spirit world: one gives offerings of cloth, tobacco, and prayers in return for blessings from the spirits. The term Sun Dance is, in fact, a misnomer, and Indians themselves refer to the rite as a "thirsting dance" or "rain dance." At the end of the ceremony, having fasted and thirsted for a vowed period of up to four days, the participants one by one approach the lodge's center pole, weeping and wailing, and lean forearm and head on it. This symbolizes the dependence of humans on the spirits—a request that they return rain and good fortune in place of the offerings made by the worshipers. At the conclusion of the ceremony, a feast is held for participants, onlookers, and guests from other reserves. Following this, such things as money and blankets (provided out of a fund contributed to by band members) are presented to visitors, accompanied by elaborate speeches.

It is expected that all giving and receiving on the reserve take place freely, but there are numerous occasions when this does not happen. The rule of generosity may either be flagrantly broken or be sidestepped. The following is a typical episode:

Charlie Deersleep came to my tent late one night as I was preparing for bed. He had a six-pack of beer under his jacket, and carefully stashed it beside my firewood. We talked for a short time, exchanging pleasantries, and he asked if I wanted a beer. I accepted, and he removed two bottles from his supply. We continued to talk about the States, job opportunities there, etc. In a few minutes, I was startled by two young Antelope brothers, who emerged from the darkness into the light of the fire. Charlie made moves to hide the bottle he'd just emptied behind him. The two Antelopes sat down, and a tense quarter-hour followed: i.e., "I know that you know what I got." But only small talk took place, the two waiting to be offered a drink. Finally, they stood up and started to walk off, George saying bitterly, "Come on, Gordon, that stingy sonofabitch ain't gonna give us a lick off the bottle cap."

Such outbursts are unusual. More commonly, the Indian who possesses something simply takes pains to conceal it, the rule being that any visible resource may legitimately be requested by another. One afternoon, when I was not at home, my wife recorded:

Violet Antelope came by, and asked me to keep some money for her. She said, "I'm gonna town, an' I don't want to take it all. Otherwise, they'll get it" (i.e., her companions, whom she had asked to wait outside). She proceeded to empty the contents of each pocket, her bra, her shoes, and her cigarette pack, coming up with a total of about thirty dollars, of which she gave me twenty. She explained, as she was assembling her cash, "If you keep it all in one place, then they'll know how much you got."

Sometimes, the concealment desired can require elaborate deception. For example, at one time a few Indians had the habit of secreting liquor in lockers at the railway depot, saving it for later. When this was discovered, other band members began to hang out nearby, so that they could keep track of those who entered the station. This safe depository then had to be abandoned.

As with so many events on the reserve, matters can sometimes take a comical turn. Tony Dumont related to me the consequences of his attempts to protect a cache from his wife:

Tony, as he related, came back late from town, and had managed to get home with two six-packs of beer and a fifth of wine. The wine he stashed outside the house. He hid one six-pack under the bed (knowing it would be the first place she would look), and the other in the oven [of their wood-burning stove]. He figured that she would find the first six-pack and be satisfied with that, leaving the rest for him. He then went to bed. Sometime in the middle of the night, Margaret got up, found the beer and drank it, and went back to sleep. In the morning, Tony was awakened by a violent explosion. "I thought the whole goddamned house was coming down," he said. It seemed that his kids had got up before them and, not knowing what was secreted in the oven, had built a fire to make some pancakes. The beer heated, exploded, and scared the hell out of Tony. He said, "You shoulda seen it; it blew the door off the oven, and there was broken glass all over the place. But nobody got hurt. The kids had already finished eatin' and gone outside. . . . I was glad I hid the wine outside. At least I had that left for Sunday."

A more serious infraction of the requirement to share, especially when taken in the context of its aboriginal significance, concerns the office of band chief. Gordon Bullrobe had been elected chief by the band about a year before my second arrival. The office rotates among the adult men, has no authority over the rest of the band, and is not especially sought by the incumbent. During the summer of my stay, however, a rancher negotiated with Gordon to cut some hay on the reserve, for which he paid Gordon $300. Instead of turning this sum over to the band fund or distributing it to others, Gordon used it for repairs to his truck and a trip to a reserve in the east. Although he was never overtly confronted with his "embezzlement," there was considerable resentment among other band members, some of whom began plotting his removal as chief.[1]

The issues that generate conflict on the reserve are not always small or trivial ones. For example, the band's land is held jointly and has not been parceled out into individual holdings. Indians will cut posts, make hay, or use other resources as they are needed. Johnny and Gordon Antelope, however, ran into some difficulties:

Gordon told me that he was worried about having enough hay to get through the winter. Last fall, he and his brother had plowed up a 50-acre tract on the bench in order to improve the hay crop. They put a lot of work into it. Then, without saying anything, Archie Russell contracted with Jimmy Dant [a White rancher] to put up the hay from that field on shares. Both brothers were exceedingly resentful of the maneuver; they had counted on that feed. Gordon was all the more angry because Archie has no cattle to feed, and will just sell his share of the bales.

---

[1] One band member, in the minority, expressed a somewhat different view of the matter: "Well, we knew Gordon got the money . . . but he was havin' trouble with his truck and his wife, so we never said anything. . . . After all, it is his turn at chief."

I asked him why he didn't protest or try to stop the deal, and he said, "Well, there's nothin' I could say, he just got to it before us."

Occasionally, one can observe open outbursts of resentment at having to share. Shortly before the town stampede, a group of Indians and myself were standing at the sidelines:

Delbert Deersleep took a cigarette from his pack, and Jimmy Deersleep, standing next to him, put out his hand for a smoke. Jimmy took one, and handed the pack to the next man on the right.... The pack made it around the circle and returned to Delbert nearly empty. Delbert blew up, threw what was left on the ground, said, "There, take 'em *all*, you bunch of leeches," and stomped off.[2]

It should be added that at this stampede an Indian had contracted with the White director to stage a "genuine" Indian wagon race with first, second, and third prizes in cash. Four wagons and teams were entered, and, although the organizer won, he split the money evenly among all the contestants.

There are other ways in which the expectation to share—and criticism for failure to do so—are displayed. Resentment is often expressed against band members who attempt to "get ahead," and those who seek to better their lot as individuals are thought to be selfish and swellheaded. For example, Gordon Antelope had worked nearly four years for the highway department, abandoning his house on the reserve for a small but comfortable one on the edge of town. For most of the period of his employment, he complained, he was constantly besieged by Indians who expected to be fed and put up for overnight or longer, or who asked to borrow his clothes, his money, or his car. His fellow band members, in return, complained of his stinginess, and of his practice of not answering the door and pretending to be out. Occasional criticism was directed at him openly, when he would be told to "stop tryin' to act like a big shot." Although Gordon finally decided to give up his job and return home, his and his brother's joint cattle venture continued to bring him criticism (see Chapter 3).

[2] Similarly, an Indian man told me that it is better to smoke roll-your-owns. "Ready-mades taste better; but if they got to roll 'em themselves, people won't ask you so much for tobacco, and when they do it's cheaper anyway."

Occasionally, Indians will show resentment toward friends whom they feel have misused them in the matter of sharing. Tony Dumont, reflecting on the past and on his present state, speculated:

When I got that money [his inheritance] everybody was my friend. There was always a bunch followin' me around. But when it was all spent they cleared out. Now I got to be careful, watch my step around here. . . . Like, old Charlie [Antelope, Tony's father-in-law] was worried about what's gonna happen to his cattle when he dies, and he asked me to take care of them, said he'd give them to me. But I said I couldn't do that. . . . The others would get jealous, think I was gettin' too big, and kick me off the reserve. Sometimes I think if I ever got on my feet again, they'd break me. I know what would happen. . . . I'd think, "Oh, hell, they like me, I better give 'em something." And then I'd have nothin' all over again.

Another young man, Harry Beaver, was married to an attractive Short Grass girl, whom he had met while she was visiting his home reserve several hundred miles to the east. They divided their time between the two reserves; and on one occasion, having worked on potato farms in the east for several months, they purchased an old car and returned to Short Grass. Harry, too, thought that he had been taken: "We spent about $150 in Burke partying before we left, and got here with over $200. When we got here, we started partying again, and that money was gone in three or four days. . . . It really went fast." Harry felt that people would not have had much use for him if he hadn't had a car. Later, after the vehicle had run out of gas, he left it in town, selling two of its tires for a dollar apiece. Concluding that he was not going to be "paid back" —that is, reciprocally supported by the other Short Grass band members—he left the reserve, hitchhiking back home alone.

Stingy People

Most evasions of the duty of sharing occur primarily in the concealment of resources, and rarely does anyone directly refuse a request for something. Those who are considered to be overly selfish are invariably labeled with the epithet "stingy"—and indeed, I found this term used to characterize unpopular people in general. I have already mentioned one man on the reserve who was somewhat of an outcast. He was disliked by most band members, suspected of being a police "informer," and thought to practice "bad medicine." However, the most frequent disapproval I heard expressed was that he was stingy.

But this criticism is not reserved exclusively for Indians who have not kept their obligations. Again and again, Whites were described in this manner. During one of my conversations with John Bullrobe, we sat in front of his house, from which point we could see a White rancher stacking bales of hay about a mile farther down the hills. John remarked: "Look at him, working himself to death for those stupid cattle! He's got plenty of money, I'll tell you. What does he do when he gets all that money? Nothin'! He just sits on it. He wouldn' give you a dime if you asked him, even if you was starvin'. He stingy, just like the rest of 'em [White men]."

Ranchers and farmers, Indian agents, and townspeople are similarly condemned. And Indians seem to apply the same standards or expectations regarding generosity to themselves and to Whites. One Saturday afternoon,

John Deersleep stopped Donald Cook in town and asked him for the "loan" of two dollars. Donald refused, but John kept pressing, not accepting Donald's refusals. John said, "I know you got it, you're rich. I ain't got nothin', so you got to give me the money. Come on." Donald, obviously growing angry, again flatly refused, and walked away. John came back to where we were standing, muttering about the "stingy bastard."

That Whites are miserly and unwilling to extend help, is a frequently verbalized source of Indian disapproval. In fact, for the band members this is a major distinction between themselves and Whites. One Indian man put it this way:

I tell you, the White man has got his religion, and the Indian has his, thatsa difference. Thatsa way it should be. The White God is no good for the Indian, don't listen to him [the Indian]. . . . White men are stingy. They don't take care of anybody, just take care of themselves. Indians different. We care for each other, share what we got. Nobody ever goes hungry as long as somebody else has got something to eat. We take care of each other up here. We all take pity on each other, and we help each other. Thatsa difference.

Earlier, I raised the issue of the Indians' threatened sense of identity when confronted with a White denial of their value as persons. It would appear that sharing is seized upon as one means of rescuing a measure of self-esteem. Among themselves, Indians can point to their generosity as morally worthy—and in fact as rendering them morally superior to Whites. There are, of course, other ways in which they claim that this is so: for instance, Indians believe their religion transcends Christianity, and that unlike Whites, they are not hypocritical about their religion. Still, the quality of generosity and willingness to share that Indians attribute to themselves is perhaps the single strongest source of their self-image, which is confirmed and validated to them each time a White refuses to meet some request. Further proof comes from the always visible affluence of Whites, which is taken to indicate White acquisitiveness.

Even though the ideal of sharing is often not realized on the reserve, as when Indians conceal things or share grudgingly, it remains a prominent one in Indian thought. And its usefulness in constructing a morally defensible image of self seems enough to insure its persistence, no matter what the inconvenience. Moreover, the force of the conviction that Indians share and Whites do not is enough to mask for Indians the distinctly un-Indian behavior of some band members. That is, when an Indian avoids sharing, he is not defined as White by his fellows; to be sure, he will have committed a breach of the ideal, but he will not be judged in the same way as a White man.

For Indians, the values of generosity and reciprocity also provide grounds for explaining their present plight. They see their deprivation as a result of the White man's avarice and stinginess in controlling natural resources. This judgment was often expressed when I asked Indians for opinions on their history. Of the nineteenth-century treaties one man said:

I'll tell you what happened. The Queen's men came and brought us rum. We never had that before and did not know what it could do to you. . . . It can make you drunk so that you do things you don't want to do. So, they called all of the chiefs together, and after they gave them lots of rum, they read them this paper and asked if Whites could come and live here with us. The chiefs, they did not know what that meant, so they said yes and signed the paper. They welcomed the White man to come. They thought there was plenty for everybody, they thought that Indians and Whites would help each other. And then Whites took everything, and they killed all our buffalo. They left us nothing but this little Indian land. And now they treat us bad. We have to beg from the agent for anything we need.

In other words, the White man violated the principle of reciprocity. In exchange for the Indians' generosity and hospitality, White settlers gave nothing in return. Worse than that: in exchanges, Indians expect that the person with the greatest wealth ought to be the most generous; but the White man did not even return the Indians' gifts in equal quantity. Thus the generosity ethic explains the past as well as the present to Indians, to their moral advantage. Undoubtedly this feeling on the part of Short Grass Indians is at the root of their usual attitudes toward the Indian Affairs Branch and the aid they expect from that agency.

So far, I have spoken of sharing and generosity from the Indian perspective. Whites are aware of Indian behavior in this regard and have, in turn, put the sharing ideal to work in the interest of their own moral superiority. A rancher reported:

As long as there was a schoolteacher on the reserve, he supervised a deal between Joe Abbott and the band in which Joe grew oats on Indian benchland. This was done on a share basis, fifty-fifty, and the teacher saw to it that the band's share was distributed evenly among Indian families. Now that there is no teacher, other arrangements have been made. In '66, Alex Lewis agreed to sow and harvest 50 acres for Charlie Antelope, in exchange for repairs to his fences. Asked if he was doing it on shares, Alex said, "Hell no!" . . . He wasn't going to get involved in a share deal with Indians and in the kinds of complications that always arise.

Bob Mills said that four years ago he made a deal with Charlie Scarbelly to sow 100 acres in oats for winter feed in return for Charlie's labor. Bob agreed, and Charlie was able to store quite a bit for the winter. The next year, Bob asked Charlie if he wanted to repeat the deal, and Charlie said no. Charlie said that he had wound up with very little of the oats for himself, and that other Indians came to get feed for their horses whenever they needed it, and he had to give it to them. Bob did not approve of the sharing business. In his view, all those oats were Charlie's rightful property, and he had worked hard for them. He did not think it fair that the others benefited from Charlie's labor—"The lazy bastards."

A rancher who periodically hired Indians who came to live on his place said:

I used to think that they had some sort of communal thing going on up there. You know, where they help each other out and share things. But I was wrong about that: they're really a greedy bunch, out for anything they can get. And once a guy is outta money, they got no use for 'im any more. I've seen it so many times here. They'd come by when they knew he was getting paid, and want him to go to town drinking with them. And, of course, he'd go, and his money would be gone in nothing flat. And damn if they would even give him a ride back here. The next morning he'd call up and ask me to come and get him. I hated to even pay the poor bastard, knowin' that the others would wind up with the money. Same way with Wilbert and Gordon, and with every other Indian who ever worked here. . . . The trouble with hiring Indians is that you can't hire just one of 'em; you wind up with the whole crowd.

Another man, whose ranch was near the reserve, talked about a stroke that Charlie Antelope had suffered a year previously:

Charlie's sons started fighting over his stuff as soon as he was gone. They sold one of his horses, and I saw 'em hauling some of his hay to town to sell. All this time, old Charlie is lying in the hospital wondering where in the hell he's gonna get another 600 bales to winter his cattle, and they're selling what little bit he's got. You know, old Charlie really looks after those boys. I seen him sell a cow to bail 'em out of jail. When one of 'em rolled his truck and totaled it, he just bought another one, sold another cow. What does he get for it? They don't seem to care for him at all. They didn't even wait to see if he died before they started grabbin' his property.

To Whites, then, Indians are poor because they exploit one another. Indian sharing is regarded as little more than an expression of Indian greed—once again, a respect in which Indians are morally inferior to Whites. Indians lack incentive because they will not break out of a relationship in which they are deprived by their fellows. And Whites regard evasions and infractions of sharing on the part of Indians, as well as the communalism that does prevail, as indications of Indians' essential selfishness and moral failure. This greed, not exploitation by Whites, is the reason for Indian poverty. Sharing is seen by Whites as a part of the Indians' general proclivity to "bunch up." As long as single Indians or families refuse to strike out on their own, they will remain in the same rut. Frank Pope and other Whites, for example, saw this as the reason for Tony Dumont's failure and pressed him to disengage himself from other Indians, even to the point of suggesting that he leave his wife. The same train of thought was expressed to me by George Suggs, a town councilor who was concerned about the "Indian problem."

He knew that sooner or later Indians would start moving to town, and he wanted to avoid the development of an "Indian slum." He had been in communication with the IAB to "do something," but he was at a loss himself about how to proceed. It was clear that he wanted Indians to become responsible, upstanding citizens before they became town dwellers. As he said, "We want them here on our terms, not on theirs."

One thing he was sure of: the adults are "beyond help," since they mutually support one another's delinquency. Suggs thinks that it is the children of grammar-school age who have to be worked on. If they can be drawn into White peer groups, they will develop ambitions to better themselves. For him, education is the answer: "If we can teach them to read and write, then at least they've got that . . . if we can get an Indian through grade five or six, I don't see how he could ever go back to the kind of life the rest of them lead."

Suggs even suggested that the only way to "save" the children was to get them away from the influence of their parents and place them separately in White homes. Doubtful about the feasibility of this, he said, "If we could just start some kind of boarding school or something, anything to get them away from that place."

Two further observations can be made here (though I shall return to them later). I have mentioned the failure of the Hudson's Bay Traders to comprehend the ritual component of their exchanges with Indians. But even though Indians and traders misunderstood one another's actions, they were still able to establish relatively stable relations. To Indians, the exchanges meant one thing, to Whites another; yet this did not impede or preclude the trading of furs for guns. Similarly, the sharing ethic is turned by both Indians and Whites to their respective moral advantage. It explains the affluence of Whites and the poverty of Indians, and it validates for each group the moral inferiority of the other.

My final point concerns the study of "values." Customarily, social scientists have regarded values as ends in themselves, as goal-oriented guidelines for human action. Values are a part of the culture that shapes human action, and, directly or indirectly, they reflect ways of organizing societal energy. But when we examine the "value" of sharing in Indian-White interactions, an additional possibility arises. Values can come to be objects—that is, items that are subject to a sort of manipulation in which they become something more than guides to action. In the case of Short Grass, they are used to mold a self in which pride can be taken, and at the same time to defend against moral assaults on that self.

THUS FAR, I have examined several strategies used by Indians to adapt to their social and moral status in the Short Grass community. Assimilative strategies, which are relatively ineffective, occur together with retreat from White society, with a search for approval, and with the development of a morally worthy self-image within the reserve subcommunity. Now I turn to a third mode of orientation, one that involves both the rejection of White behavioral norms by Indians and the overt acknowledgment by Indians of their profane character. I refer to the Indians' practice of "victimizing" Whites—of capitalizing on their profaneness in order to win immediate small gains of money and other resources or services. Many of the events discussed in this chapter are of the same general nature as others described previously (especially in Chapter 5). But I now wish to examine them with an eye to the ways in which Indians exploit their moral status and knowledge of White society for gain, keeping in mind that this tactic clearly reinforces Indian profaneness in the eyes of Whites. Exploitation does not take place in one direction only, to be sure, and Whites take advantage of Indians in various ways. It is instructive to begin by looking at some of these.

Conning the Con Man

As I have indicated, Short Grass Whites define a worthy man as one who, among other things, possesses unquestioned integrity. For them, one's word is a sacred thing. In fact, many economic transactions between ranchers, or between ranchers and mer-

chants, are negotiated with no more security than a man's word
and a handshake. But the Whites' emphasis on integrity and charity is not always discernible in their transactions with Indians. For
example, Indians who do not own trucks and want to haul fenceposts to town for sale often hire a White trucker to do the job. The
posts are loaded and unloaded by the Indian, and for his small
investment in time, little more than an hour, the White sometimes charges as much as 25 percent of the load's value. One man
regularly goes into the lumberyard office to collect his fee from
the manager while his Indian customer unloads the posts, apparently believing that he has to pocket his money before the Indian
gets his hands on it. Similarly, the rancher who for several years
operated a small "Indian store" on his place near the reserve often
took posts in payment for merchandise; but the value of the goods
he sold in this way was usually considerably lower than the same
load of posts would have fetched in town. He, of course, sold the
posts to other ranchers at a handsome profit.

Whites frequently take advantage of the official restrictions
placed on Indian sale of reserve resources. The law forbids Indians
to sell cattle without the permission of the Indian agent, and to
circumvent this, Indians often sell cattle to Whites surreptitiously
and for less than their market value. Similarly, some ranchers take
advantage of the Indians' desire for ready spending money by
arranging to graze their cattle on the reserve pastureland for much
less than they would have to pay if they went through legal channels. The grazing fees are supposed to go into a common band
fund rather than to individual Indians, but they do not.[1] Indians
also sell hay in violation of regulations. An agent reported:

I know that they are selling the stuff, but I can never catch 'em. George
Russell was hauling hay into town and selling it for fifty cents a bale. . . .
Hell, they could of got a dollar for them standing in the field. But nobody
[i.e. no White man] would be willing to risk getting caught hauling it
off the reserve. The next time I see 'em going to town with hay you can
bet I'll turn that truck around so fast they won't know what happened.

---

[1] While there was a teacher on the reserve, these activities were more clandestine. The last teacher wrote letter after letter to the IAB, complaining about
specific ranchers who were trucking cattle off the reserve after dark. Nothing,
however, was done about this.

Transactions between band members and Whites have a way of becoming extraordinarily involved. For example, a rancher agreed to grow hay on Indian land on shares, on a 50–50 basis. Another man struck the same bargain with a different Indian, precipitating a lively dispute that ended when the two Whites came to blows in a town cafe. It was a third rancher who finally put up the crop. Although the principals did not think so, the whole affair was a source of great amusement to both Indians and Whites.

In another case, a rancher made a deal with Chief Gordon Bullrobe to grow winter feed on Indian land, again on shares. He did this one year and expected the same arrangement to continue the next year. But after the two Antelope brothers began their cattle business they decided to use the land themselves (with the approval of the band council). The rancher became incensed at this, having developed a proprietary attitude to the land. He felt that since he had "improved" the plot, he had the right to continue using it: "I put up *seven* miles of fence up there. . . . Besides, it's a month too late to put up oats anyway." In his opinion, then, Indians could neither manage the land competently nor use the harvest effectively.

Whites exploit many opportunities to cash in on reserve affairs. At the time I was preparing to leave in the spring of 1967 the reserve was being wired for electricity by a local firm, with the IAB paying the bill. The owner of the firm told a rancher that he was going to "wire everything in sight, and charge 'em plenty." He proceeded to do just this, installing wiring in houses that had not been occupied for several years and would not be in the future.

In town, Indians frequently pay more for goods and services than do Whites, although it is difficult to determine how extensively this takes place. In this connection, some merchants and Indians have found a way to circumvent the IAB's policies on Indian welfare aid. As noted earlier, Indians do not always receive cash payments but are sometimes credited with merchandise at a store of their choosing. It was reported to me that some managers routinely return cash kickbacks to Indians who have chosen to deal with them in this way. The store gets regular business, and the Indian receives occasional small sums of cash. The arrangement does not always work smoothly: when an Indian makes what a storekeeper sees as an excessive demand, an argument usually results, and sometimes the Indian will take his patronage elsewhere.

No civic or religious organization in Short Grass extends charity of any sort to Indians. The prevailing White opinion, in fact, is that Indians already receive more assistance than they deserve. Individual Whites sometimes do small favors for Indians, but even then the outcome of their charity is often a negative one, as evidenced by one man's experience. For a time, John Deersleep had a small house in town, which was eventually condemned by the town council and for which he paid $25 a month. The place was without electricity and running water, and one of the two rooms had a dirt floor. John, a man in his early sixties, lived there with four of his grandchildren so that they could attend school more regularly than would have been possible if they had to rely on the school bus to the reserve. There were also usually one or two other adult Indians staying there. The house was in a poor state of repair and, without water, difficult to keep clean. After the house was condemned, John was told to vacate it and began looking for another. One of the town councilors, James Dant, who had been among a group of Whites concerned about Indian housing in town, made up a bundle of old clothes discarded by his wife and took them to John. After the visit, I asked Dant if he knew of some place John could rent. He said, "Absolutely not! I wouldn't help him move onto anybody's property, the condition that place was in. It is filthy. . . . I wouldn't give 'em a coal shed to live in."

Though not all Whites engage in these and similar practices, those who do are not publicly or privately censured by other Whites. Neither do White members of the community comment on the less direct deprivations suffered by Indians. The legal and political status of Indians is of course a matter of Canadian government policy. But Whites have made no efforts to bring about policy changes that might give Indians greater self-sufficiency, nor have they taken any local community action to provide Indians with such things as occupational skills or agricultural training. In fact, as we have seen, Short Grass Whites blame Indians themselves, not legal status, for Indian difficulties.

In a community where standards of honesty and humaneness are prized, the exploitation and deprivation of a segment of that community is a manifest anomaly. It is not out of place to ask how the White conceptions of self that incorporate these values also incorporate contravening behavior and attitudes. One compensatory alternative for Whites is to enforce the social distance of Indians. This amounts to ignoring that an irregularity exists, or even that Indians exist. To a certain extent, the White members of the Short Grass community take this solution. For instance, my examination of back issues of the weekly Short Grass newspaper, for its 60-year history, revealed that apart from mentions of Indians in the police court column there was no recognition whatever that an Indian reserve exists near the town.

It is impossible, of course, for Short Grass Whites to ignore the presence and condition of Indians at all times. But there are other aspects of the White bearing toward Indians that reveal how some apparent value contradictions are resolved for Whites. To identify these, it is useful to consider some of the ways that Indians "con" White men.

Wits' End

Short Grass Indians find one source of income in the poplar fenceposts they manufacture, which are soaked in a preservative for a few hours. Sometimes an impatient Indian will paint the posts with laundry bluing instead and then sell them to an unsuspecting White. Another quick way of getting money is to sell a quantity of posts sight unseen, telling the buyer that they are stacked at some spot on the reserve. When the White returns later, having found no posts, the Indian innocently conjectures that "someone musta stole 'em." Again, Indians are able to stack posts for White buyers in such a way that there appear to be more than there actually are. There seems to be no end to the means Indians devise to get the better of Whites. A rancher told me:

I made a deal with old Charlie for 600 posts and paid him part in advance. He finally came here and said they were all stacked and ready to go, that I had better pick 'em up quick before somebody got to 'em. Well, I didn't go up to the reserve until the next day, and goddamn if there wasn't only but 500 left. That's 20 bucks I'm out and won't ever see again. You gotta watch them buggers careful.

The con game played by Indians against Whites often is carried out in the context of enduring relationships. For example, Sam Timber receives a $70 monthly disability check from the government. Each month, he takes part of this sum to the owner of an appliance store in town to hold for him, with the understanding that he can request small amounts of it at any time. By the end of every month Sam has overdrawn his "allowance," and the financial state of affairs between him and his banker is hopelessly confused, as it has been for years. In effect, Sam has a reliable, permanent source of spending money. The storekeeper laments: "I really don't know any more how much he owes me, and I probably never will. What can I do? If I don't take care of him, he'll probably starve."

Incidents of Indians duping Whites occur with almost monotonous regularity. An Indian will call at the home of an absent White man and tell the housewife that her husband has told him to get from her several dollars owed for some work done; when the husband returns, his wife discovers he has not seen this Indian in weeks, and that the payment was for an imaginary task. An Indian will persuade a White to transport him and his family home in sub-zero weather for some agreed price. When they arrive at the reserve, the Indian proclaims that he "hasn't got the money now" and will pay later, which means never. A common way for Indians to borrow money is to offer some item as security—a piece of clothing or household utensil—and then never return to claim it or to pay the debt. A rancher reported:

Oscar Lodgeskins brought by a saddle and wanted me to loan him twenty bucks on it, and I said okay. He never said anything more about it, even though I asked him a couple of times for the money. And then, about a month later, Billy Russell comes by and says where's his saddle? He said that Oscar borrowed it from him. Well, I finally gave it to him, but I know I'll never see the money from Oscar.

One of the most celebrated recent coups concerned the illegal sale of a water pump and windmill by several Indians to a neighboring rancher, who paid for the machinery and the steel tower on which it was mounted without first obtaining a permit from the Indian agent. The rancher and his son disassembled their purchase and took it home. That night, the same Indians collected the tower and pump, hauled them into town, and sold them the next day to a junk dealer.

In these transactions, Whites do not complain to the police when they suffer losses, even when there is "proof" that Indians are the malefactors. A rancher from whom Indians had poached chickens told me, "They know that all they have to do is ask me for 'em if they were really hungry, but they'd rather steal 'em." Similarly, ranchers who believe that Indians have cut timber off their land, or have stolen posts already prepared by the rancher, do not report these incidents to the police.

Indians sometimes engage in collusion with unscrupulous Whites to beat the system. The following incident related by a retired rancher is typical.

This happened about two years ago. . . . You know, I built most of those houses up there myself in '57, eight of 'em. They had got sort of run down, windows out of plumb and so on. There was some where doors were missing, and where walls was torn out, I don't know why. Anyway, the agent and me had a talk about my contracting to do the repairs. I went up there and spent two days just figuring the materials, and made up a order list.

Well, Leonard Deersleep and a couple of the other boys decided that they wanted to do it, and they talked to the agent about it. They figured that *they* had the right to the pay, since they're Indians, and they ought to work on Indian houses. I knew damn well what was happening, and I warned him [the agent was in this case a man not familiar with the community]. But the government does have a policy of self-help or something; and as long as they asked, they had first choice on the job.

Finally, a truckload of stuff went up from Garrick's [lumberyard]. You know, plywood and two-by-fours, some roofing, and fittings and hardware. Of course, the work never got done, and all those materials just vanished. . . . I've got a pretty good idea where it went, over to [a small village nearby]. I bet anything they had the whole deal arranged from the beginning, but Michaels [the agent] was just too dumb to listen to me. But he was hopping mad about it later when he found out what happened. Them houses still need work, of course.

A similar episode was reported to me by a number of Whites. After receiving several complaints from ranchers, an agent supplied some Indians with materials to make much-needed repairs to the fencing surrounding the reserve. These materials also vanished; and in the end the ranchers did the repairs themselves, sending a bill for materials and labor to the IAB.

Panhandling

"Borrowing" money has become a problem in Short Grass, and many Whites complain that they cannot walk down the streets without being "pestered" by Indians. The usual approach is to ask several persons for small amounts until a desired sum is collected. One White woman complained about this, adding, "They've even started asking people they don't know for money, complete strangers." It was bad enough, she thought, that Indians would make requests of Whites they knew; but to ask for money indiscriminately (and she thought this a recent development) was a sign of their increasing loss of self-respect.

Most of this borrowing goes on under the pretext of depositing some article of value as security, and the process sometimes gets complicated. A retired rancher recounted two such incidents.

Charlie Deersleep pawned a rifle to me with no bolt—said he'd bring it in later, and never did. That was months ago. That gun's just no use to me at all. And his brother came in not long ago and pawned another gun. That one's a dandy little rifle, and I don't care if he comes back for it, I'd just as soon keep it.

About two weeks ago, Margaret Antelope came to our door, wantin' money. We could smell on her breath that she'd been drinkin' wine. I told her no. Then she started to unbutton her shirt and said she'd pawn it to me for $3. I tell you, I was so tickled—that she wanted to give me the shirt off her back—that I gave it to her and told her to "keep her shirt on."

Such pawning goes on in public places as well:

In the pub, Wilbert Antelope, fresh out of money, approached Frank Pope [for whom he occasionally works]. He was wearing a belt with very nice beadwork in it. Without saying anything, he took it off, handed it to Frank, and asked for the loan of $2. Frank said, "I don't want none of your clothes; keep the thing, and I'll *give* you 50 cents."

The pubs in Short Grass seem to be the scene of more or less constant attempts to panhandle, since they are establishments where Indians spend a great deal of time and frequently run out of funds. I have even seen Indians offer to sell their boots to some White; most often, requests are made directly for loans, which are rarely repaid. Whites have come to expect such touches:

A farmer came into the pub, and Gordon Deersleep was sitting at a table near the door. He called to the man to come over to his table; but the man pretended not to hear, and proceeded quickly across the room to a table where several other men were sitting.

In the pub, Tony says to a White man who has just entered, "Hey, Sam! Come over here." Sam, not yet seated, was standing about 15 feet away. He said, "I'm happy right where I am." Tony countered with, "Don't be a hermit. Come over here. I want to talk with you about somethin'." Sam moves a little closer, seemingly in spite of himself. It is difficult to ignore such invitations. Tony says, "Come closer." Sam replies, "I'm close enough now; I can hear you. What do you want this time?" He sits down one table away from Tony, and shows resolve not to move any closer. Tony begins to falter, and appears ready to move to Sam's table. Sam is saved when he is joined by another White man who enters and joins him, the two entering a huddle at the table.

The following is a good illustration of patterned "borrowing" on the part of Indians:

Begging. Louis Scarbelly's performance in the pub this afternoon. He would call Whites over to his table as they entered the place. The effect of this, when successful, is to put the victim in Indian territory and in a defensive position. Louis's requests are made in hushed tones, and his marks break away from the encounter only with discomfort and difficulty. In some cases, he would ask the person to enter the men's room with him, or he would follow someone into the men's room. The advantage of that technique is that the payoff is concealed from Whites as well as from other Indians. Also, characteristically, Louis will not accept excuses—e.g., that the person doesn't have any money—and he does not give up with the first refusal. He tries to keep the mark engaged, to block attempted retreats.

Parenthetically, one man told me of a defensive technique to meet such requests for money:

When I see one of 'em in the pub and it looks like a touch is comin', *I* ask 'em *first* to pay me back some money, two or three bucks. It doesn't make any difference if that particular Indian doesn't really owe it to me— they never remember these things anyhow. But it helps you get the jump on 'em, and if they think you're gonna press them for the money, they'll back off.

Indians have discovered that some persons are in a better position to ask for money than others. When a car full of Indians stops at a White house to borrow money, one of the younger women is always sent in rather than a man, since she will have a better chance of getting it than would a man. This does not work in public places, however. A rancher said: "You got to be careful givin' Indian women money on the street or any place people can see you. You know what they'd make of that." It also happens that Indians, seeing that a White is reluctant to pay up, will threaten a "scene." In the grocery store,

Bullrobe was at the checkout corner with Charlotte Antelope, who had a small pile of groceries to be charged to her account. Bullrobe also wanted $10 to be charged to his. The checker refused, saying that he had already given him enough money that month. Bullrobe was obviously getting angry, and began to raise his voice. "That's my money," he said, "and I want it." The manager looked nervously around the store and noticed that people were beginning to watch. He turned back to Bullrobe and said softly, "Okay, okay. I'll do it this time, but no more this month."

When they see that a white man is cornered, Indians will press their requests until the victim pays just to get rid of them. One evening I accompanied Charlie and Helen Deersleep (both in their early fifties) into a small grocery store. Helen, who had been drinking moderately, was intent on securing the loan of enough gas money for a trip to a reserve in the east. She and the wife of the proprietor were not personally acquainted.

There were two customers sitting at the soda fountain, but the place was otherwise empty. All the time, these two never looked toward the checkout counter to acknowledge what was happening there. The woman at the counter herself would occasionally lapse into absorption with some small task, ignoring Helen and trying to break off the transaction. Charlie and I stood a few paces away, intently studying the contents of shelves.

Helen first asked for $15. She said, "My little baby is sick; I gotta have money to make her well." The woman made various excuses— that she didn't have the money, that her husband would be mad at her, that she would never get paid back. She seemed suspicious of Helen's claims about the illness, but did not challenge this [in fact, there was no sick child]. All to no avail; Helen continued to press her. The woman, looking as if she'd found an out, said, "Besides, you can't do anything now, the hospital's closed. Why don't you wait and take her in tomorrow?" Not to be outfoxed, Helen explained with great urgency that the child had to be taken to Moose Mountain—that there was nobody here to treat her unusual affliction, which Helen began to describe in detail.

Finally, after twenty minutes, the proprietress, seeing that she couldn't outdo Helen, offered a dollar. Then the bargaining began, and Helen finally worked the amount up to $6, which she took.

Incorrigible Indians

Why, one may ask, do Whites cheated by Indians keep coming back for more? Why is an Indian "lent" money when all past experience must demonstrate that it most probably will never be returned? One outcome of the usual sequence of events in a con is that the "mark" learns from his mistakes: he presumably is a poorer but a more cautious man. In fact, Short Grass Whites *expect* to be conned by Indians; and the effect of each such incident is that Indian irresponsibility and childishness is demonstrated and confirmed. When a rancher pays an Indian in advance to stack bales of hay and the Indian does not show up for work, the rancher's image of the Indian as irresponsible is validated. His tolerance of the social deprivation of Indians can then be given a rationale like: "They are irresponsible children. They are not really men, so they cannot be expected to participate in the adult world." Similarly, those Whites who directly exploit Indians preserve a consistent image of self: "Sure, he takes advantage of me, but that is to be expected of children. I graze my cattle on his land, but I am the one who takes care of him, who gives him money and sees that he does not starve." Not a few Short Grass Whites are persuaded that Indians have no desire to play White roles. A veterinarian claimed, "The last thing they want is to live like White men—they're no more than unemployed buffalo hunters, and happy just like they are."

Looking at these transactions from an Indian point of view, we encounter an interesting point. Most Indians do not accept White judgments of their roles, their selves, or their personal worth, although they seldom openly dispute these White conceptions. Indians do not regard themselves as foolish children; on the contrary, they consider themselves rather artful and successful exploiters of White men. What they do is to represent themselves to White audiences as the sort of persons Whites take them to be, meanwhile representing themselves to other Indians as something different. In their performances before Whites, Indians' behavior acknowledges their irresponsibility; but to other Indians they are seen as turning to account mistaken White opinions. This attitude is not unlike one that Ralph Ellison (1953: 7–9) describes for Negroes in the United States:

I am an invisible man. . . . That invisibility to which I refer occurs because of a peculiar disposition of the eyes of those with whom I come in contact. A matter of the construction of their *inner* eyes, those eyes with which they look through their physical eyes upon reality. I am not complaining, nor am I protesting either. It is sometimes advantageous to be unseen. . . . I remember that I am invisible and walk softly so as not to waken the sleeping ones. . . . I learned in time, though, that it is possible to carry on a fight against them without their realizing it.

White residents of Short Grass, especially those who have the fewest contacts with Indians and who are the most literate members of the community, often point to a particular novel as an accurate portrayal of Indian character. *Stay Away, Joe*, by Dan Cushman, follows the slapstick adventures of a young Indian and his friends in their con game with White society. "If you want to know what Indians are really like," they advise, "read that book—it's a scream."

Backstage, in Goffman's terminology, Indians "drop the front," and "the impression fostered by the performance is knowingly contradicted as a matter of course" (1959: 112). Jokes are made

about the gullibility of Whites, and fine points of strategy are discussed. "The way to get off easy," according to one informant,
"is to act like a dumb Indian in front of the magistrate." The punishment for being drunk or disorderly will usually be lighter than
a White would receive, and "credit" can even be arranged by
which the guilty Indian has several months to pay his fine or receives extensions on overdue fines.

Much of this backstage activity resembles that reported by Berreman for the Aleut. Aleuts, though they identify with Whites as
a valuation group, respond to their exclusion from White institutional activities by valuation group alienation. In the process of
acculturation, they have come to look more appreciatively at
White society; and, deprived of acceptance by Whites, they orient
themselves negatively toward the people whose cultural values and
goals they admire. "Role segregation" and "role distance" are two
of the means Aleuts employ to cope with this ambivalence (Berreman, 1964: 235).

Earlier, I observed that Short Grass Indians are excluded from
playing White roles, and that structural barriers prevent extensive
Indian participation in the larger society. To a greater or lesser
extent, most band members do not perform in the presence of a
White audience in a fashion suggesting that they embrace White
cultural goals. The general impression of them, in fact, is that
they are relatively "unacculturated." Nevertheless, it is evident
that they are beginning to identify positively with some aspects
of White ways of life; and in spite of the barriers to acculturation,
they show signs of having recognized White roles as desirable.
Perhaps this process has been facilitated by the similarity between
some of the principal values of traditional Plains Indian culture
and those of the Anglo-American Short Grass community. The
standards of masculinity and competitiveness, dual standards of
sexual behavior, admired qualities of leadership, and so on among
Short Grass Whites express value orientations remarkably like
those of the formerly autonomous Cree. We may expect that a
group of one cultural heritage will with greater ease identify with
a group of another when they share such values.

Many aspects of the structural relations between Whites and Indians work, or have worked, toward an acceptance by Indians of White cultural goals and meanings, if not toward complete assimilation. For one, the extermination of the buffalo and the consequent demise of the entire traditional pattern of Plains subsistence forced Indians to search elsewhere for a livelihood. And at first they were less spatially isolated than today. In the early reserve period, after the turn of the century, it was common for Indian families to live for long periods on the property of ranchers for whom they worked; and some band members were in fact born on ranches where their parents lived permanently in familiar interaction with their White employers. Modern mechanized agriculture has reduced the demand for Indian labor, but Indians still have other opportunities for exposure to White culture: all Indian women now go to the White hospital to have their children; Indian men mix with Whites in the pub; Indian children have had White schoolteachers; and Short Grass Indians maintain close relations with members of other reserves, who are more acculturated than they.

It appears that Indian children are curious about White ways and sometimes try to imitate them. Outside my tent one summer morning,

Irene Deersleep [about 13 years old] was playing "wedding" with five or six younger children. The ceremony was most elaborate. She had laid out a "church" on the ground, marking off the altar, aisle, etc., with pieces of wood, poles, and two-by-fours. Larry Deersleep [10 years] was the unwilling groom, allowing Irene to push him about, tell him where to stand, how to walk down the aisle, etc. The bride was an [8-year-old] Antelope girl. Irene had made her a bouquet of clover blossoms, carefully fixed her hair, and attached a bridal veil and a train. She had several smaller girls acting as bridesmaids. Irene rehearsed the ceremony several times, each time impatiently finding some fault with one or the other of her cast. Acting as preacher herself, she gave a pretty good approximation of the routine, e.g., "Do you, Larry Deersleep, take this woman for your lawfully wedded wife." And so on. Larry became particularly uncomfortable at the kissing part, and his bride coyly shy. Irene seemed to be willing to keep up the game all morning, but the groom deserted the scene in spite of her protests.

It is hard to say where the girl picked up her knowledge of the proceedings. She did attend the movies frequently, and, like other Indian girls her age, she was addicted to comic books that portray true love and romance.

Some of the Indians' attraction to—and ambivalence about—White society is well illustrated by their views regarding education. Few Short Grass Indians are literate in English; and of the six adults who can read and write, five are the wives of band members and were raised on other reserves. However, although a few Indians express small interest in education for their children, in most reserve families at least one parent wishes the youngsters to learn English and get an education. Indians, having been told by Whites for a century that education is the only way to get ahead, often insist (perhaps unrealistically) that this is the case. In fact, after the reserve school closed the band chief, at the suggestion of others, went to school officials to suggest that Indian children attend the town school.

But desirable as a magical "education" may be, some Indians recognize the threat that it poses to Indian customs, especially language. One Indian man in his late fifties, Oscar Lodgeskins, felt that younger Indians did not speak Cree as well as the older generation. He expected that the language would eventually disappear, and attributed this to the increasing use of English learned in schools. He also maintained that the young people did not seem enthusiastic about Indian ceremonial: none of the men under 25, for example, were learning Indian songs and chants.[2] Oscar talked regretfully about the passing of old ways but could think of no way to forestall it; although he wanted his children educated, he could not easily accept the implications of this.

Some Indians, it may be added, are embarrassed by their illiteracy. Tony Dumont has made several starts at reading, but never stuck with it. He once tried in prison, and has had several local Whites give him lessons. The reason he gives for dropping out

[2] This may not be so alarming. Though I cannot verify it, there is the strong possibility that even in the past young men participated only passively in complex ceremonies.

of Alcoholics Anonymous was that during meetings members took
turns reading to one another from AA literature, and he was afraid
that the book would be passed to him; he did not want to admit
publicly that he could not read. Indians, in fact, avoid many situations in which their illiteracy would be evident. For example, an
Indian woman who did not have a driver's license risked a ticket
and fine by regularly driving her husband's truck. When I suggested that she take the driver's test orally she declined, saying
that she would be too embarrassed to do so.

Continuous face-to-face interaction over generations leads to
some consensual definition of the situation, and it is reasonable
to expect that Indians should have incorporated into their conceptions of self some of the content of White roles. I found that
band members frequently judge their own behavior by White
standards. Most Indians, for example, voice a desire to be self-
supporting, to own land and cattle as their White neighbors do.

Saturday night: Gordon Bullrobe, his wife, and I strolled around town
this evening. Gordon, who had been hauling bales on Newcomb's ranch
for the past two days, had just come from the pub and was a little tight.
We passed Roger Chapman. Gordon said, "Hiya, Roger, how you been?"
in an expansive tone. Gordon's wife said, "Gordon, you can't talk to
those people like that." He replied, "What d'ya mean; I'm a *workin'*
man, ain't I?"

But however much Indians embrace White culture, they are denied the privilege of playing White roles. They cannot go into
business for themselves because their legal status prohibits the
accumulation of the capital necessary to engage in full-scale farming or ranching. Nor have they skills that would allow them to take
wage employment off the reserve. Consequently, Short Grass Indians are alienated from their valuation group, just as Berreman's
Aleuts are. But if they cannot be White, they must still be able
to define the self "along defensible lines" (Goffman, 1962: 493),
and they must do so in a way that will permit the validation of
this self by Whites. To the Indian, then, his irresponsible performances are not childish pranks: "Because I can trick White men
so easily, they are not as smart as they think they are. I'm the one
who's taking advantage of them. I can make a living by my wits."

We have looked at some of the ways Whites and Indians in Short Grass portray the self in the ordinary course of daily life, and we have seen how the action of each group validates the claims of the other. Indians and Whites successfully predict one another's behavior, and do so in a manner that mutually credits images of Indian and White selves. Among the consequences of these transactions, I will discuss two.

Containment

In his article "Cooling the Mark Out" (1962) Erving Goffman addresses himself to the problem of people's adaptations to failure, that is, to the ways in which individuals deal with the repudiation of the self implied by the unsuccessful fulfillment of some role. It often becomes necessary for a person whose self has suffered failure to be consoled by some other better situated person. In this way he is helped to adjust to his loss and is "cooled out"; this process is particularly important when a person is very deeply engaged in his self, and when its loss reflects upon him negatively. It sometimes happens, Goffman adds, that the various participants in a network of interaction take measures to avoid altogether the troublesome procedure of cooling out: for example, they attempt to cover up the fact that a person has failed, or that his value as an individual is negligible.

These processes may be recognized in transactions between Short Grass Whites and Indians. When their worth is denied, it is not possible for Indians to salvage much of their value in the estimation of Whites, but they can still save face in the eyes of other Indians. This is accomplished, as we have noted, when the Indian subcommunity observes one of its members making a dupe of a White man and bringing off some deception with impunity. In effect, the validation of such a transaction by Whites serves to "cool out" Indians. Few Short Grass Indians show evidence of serious personality disorganization—a consequence, I think, of Whites and Indians having found a way to avoid serious disruptions of the self. Whites, at the same time, are spared the malaise of confrontation with moral inconsistency in their own behavior.

The accepted routines of self-presentation and identification in Short Grass have consequences for stability on the structural as well as the personal level. The successful cooling out of a failed person means that he will be less likely to "raise a squawk" or to threaten the established system of social relationships. The position of Indians in Short Grass is one of subordination and deprivation, and the social-psychological dynamics of role-playing and identification there occur in a way that helps to perpetuate this castelike status system. In effect, Indians are provided an "out" allowing adjustment to a social environment that would otherwise be intolerable. The alternative to this acquiescence, of course, would be for Indians to try to alter their environment, to openly and explicitly challenge White superordination.

Nearly a hundred years ago, not far from Short Grass, a group of White traders "massacred" a party of Indian horse thieves (Sharp, 1955). A White man whose horse had been stolen by Indians, sold back to him, and then stolen again by the same Indians got up a party of armed men and attacked a camp where they believed the culprits to be hiding. The significant aspect of White ideas in this affair is that Indians were held responsible for their behavior and punishable for their deceptions. In this and numerous other instances Whites were not indulgently disposed to treat Indians as irresponsible, and the outcome was sometimes violent. Today, when representations of Indian and White selves fail, the persons involved feel embarrassed or insulted. In one case I heard of, an Indian who had inopportunely asked a White man in town for several dollars was refused and told that he was a worthless beggar incapable of properly supporting his family. The Indian was affronted and flew into a rage, and the two men exchanged blows in the street. It was not so much the refusal that produced violence as the rejection by the White of the self presented by the Indian. The normal course of interaction was disrupted when the White withdrew agreement to a definition of the situation that included an image of the Indian as uncommitted to White values and standards of responsibility.

In this chapter I have described something of the tenor of Indian-White interaction, stressing role-taking, performance, and the

self. My analysis has not been exclusively concerned with the results of Indian acculturation or the extent to which Indians
embrace White values, but has considered, as well, the involvement of these values in selves identified with Whites and Indians
vis-à-vis one another. In other words, I have emphasized the mechanisms of acculturative processes rather than the conditions of
culture contact or the larger, more abstract results of contact. As
much space has been devoted to the "how" of continued Indian
segregation—the complementary presentation of diverse self-
images—as to the "why."

Looking at the results of acculturation rather than at the daily
interactions of Whites and Indians, one might conclude that the
differences in cultural values expressed in different presentations
of self are points of tension or potential conflict. But my evidence
suggests that such a view is not entirely accurate. The different
sets of values embodied in Indian and White roles constitute an
accommodation or solution to certain conflicts, and not merely a
source of them. It is, in fact, because of the contrasting images of
Indian and White that interaction in Short Grass proceeds with
as little conflict as actually occurs.

NINE Interpretations

IN ATTEMPTING to sort through some of the more puzzling features of relations between Indians and Whites in Short Grass, several general questions take prominence. First, why have the Indians, who have experienced well over a century of contact with Whites, not become more "White"? Why has the division of the community into two categories of persons achieved such stability? Second, considering the rift in values that separates Indians and Whites, why is there so little overt evidence of conflict? Finally, in what ways is the Short Grass community similar to others, and what bearing do my observations there have on the nature of human interaction generally, especially in its moral dimension? In considering these matters, I wish to isolate several factors that appear to contribute to the status quo in Short Grass, including the nature of Indians' and Whites' respective ignorance of one another and the effects of interaction patterns in leading Indians to go along with their profane status.

A Dual Moral Universe

In preceding pages I have at times presented the Indian view of social transactions and at times shifted to the White perspective. As we have seen, even though these two visions of what's going on conflict in fundamental ways, there is a sort of order and predictability to daily life in Short Grass.[1] All along I have worked in a dramaturgical frame of analysis, believing that symbolic inter-

[1] I am deeply grateful to Norman K. Denzin for a number of suggestions incorporated in this chapter.

actionism can help in understanding how such order is possible—how complementary conceptions of self and others dovetail, whatever the apparent incompatibility.

There are, to be sure, other means of characterizing the community. One might, for instance, take a straightforward social-structural stand. The procedure then would be to describe all the various institutions that make up Short Grass society, keeping in mind their implications in the larger Canadian scheme. One would describe the political process in the community, economic arrangements, religion, and kinship, and would try to show how each is tied to the others. Included would be a discussion of the inequalities of the overall system, and the differential access to valued resources of various kinds. We would then be talking about stratification arrangements, about social class within the White subcommunity, and about the profane status of Indians.[2]

With this analysis, it would be possible to describe the dehumanizing oppression of Indians in broad terms, as J. G. Jorgensen (1971) has done for the Indians of the United States. From this point of view, one can see Indians as an exploited fragment of the urban-industrial state, which subsumes even reservation Indians as a sort of rural proletariat. Jorgensen's point is that Indians are a part of modern society—that they *are* assimilated—but that the system into which they have been drawn robs them of their fair share of its wealth. This is undeniably so. What I have tried to do, however, is to move in a little closer, in one small community, to see how this process works in the minutiae of everyday life. I have attempted to describe some of the things that transpire between Indians and Whites over and over, in many different kinds of settings. To do so involves treating the community not just as a set of interrelated institutional structures but as a moral universe—a universe that is, in this case, shot through with inconsistency, disagreement, and paradox.

Like every community, Short Grass has its unique qualities, but

[2] See Lyman and Scott (1970: 1–27) for a detailed criticism of functionalism from a symbolic-interactionist point of view. Among other shortcomings they stress the failure of functionalism to take the actors' point of view, to see social life as being shaped by goal-directed action.

there are many respects in which it resembles other Indian-White communities examined by anthropologists. Edward H. Spicer (1961: 1) has observed that in contemporary North American Indian communities, "as one goes from reservation to reservation, the feeling grows that what one sees today is what one saw not long before on some other reservation." Spicer is specifically referring to typical patterns of Whites' and Indians' adjustment to one another, and to the similar personality characteristics encountered even on reservations with differing cultural origins. What has been reported by other writers appears to confirm that these similarities are indeed widespread. I can point to several illustrative examples.

Berreman's 1964 study of an isolated Aleutian community (see Chapter 8) reveals that Aleuts have come to adopt many White values and perspectives. They identify with Whites, and they evaluate their own behavior by White standards. But Aleuts who are denied free access to White roles then display what Berreman terms role distance: before Whites, they enact White roles grudgingly, demonstrating that they have not abandoned their Aleut identities. This is one possible response to subordination, and one of the responses Short Grass Indians have also made. Though Indians at times might desire to emulate Whites, they are restrained from doing so. They do not have access to avenues of achievement in White terms, and they cannot claim White identities that would be validated by Whites. Therefore, they cut losses, openly rejecting White roles and values in favor of membership-group loyalty. This is the import, for example, of Indians' casual stance toward the work ideal—an attitude particularly irritating to most Whites. In all this, Indians are fully aware that the community's stratification arrangements have the effect, as one Short Grass man put it, of "keeping us down."

Lone Hill, another Indian community described by Edward Bruner (1956, 1961), also exhibits features found in Short Grass. Lone Hill's Mandan-Hidatsa Indians, too, are isolated physically and socially from Whites; but unlike the Short Grass band, their community is subdivided into Indians who are acculturating and

Indians who are not. Bruner shows that the two groups can be distinguished by their acceptance or rejection of Indian values, especially that of generosity. Like the Indians of Short Grass, the unacculturated Mandan-Hidatsa attend giveaway dances and unanimously extol the virtues of sharing; those who are White-oriented ridicule these practices and ideas, attributing the poverty of unacculturated Indians to them. Furthermore, as Bruner discovered (1956: 621), all the acculturated Indians in Lone Hill have had White role models: they belong to nuclear families that include a White who can be emulated, and they have parents who deliberately trained them as children to think of themselves as White. Although there have been a few marriages (or alliances) with Whites among Short Grass Indian families, there have been no cases where a White parent has lived with his or her children, and thus no cases where the children of mixed marriages have been coached in White roles.

Short Grass Indians, then, are like the unacculturated segment of the Lone Hill community. For both, there are no open channels of communication with Whites. And both "lack sufficient understanding of White ways and realistic opportunities by which they may live successfully in middle-class White society" (Bruner, 1956: 621). Bruner describes the case of one Indian man who has many counterparts in Short Grass: he would like to have entered the White world and made several abortive attempts to do so; his failure resulted from a lack of knowledge about that world and a consequent inability to realistically negotiate it.

Fred O. Gearing (1970), working from field research done nearly 20 years ago, portrays a community of Fox Indians who have little real authority over their own reservation affairs, which are ultimately decided by White officials. As a result the community suffers what Gearing calls "structural paralysis." There is a social structure with nowhere to go, nothing to do; Fox men, in other words, have no opportunity to make decisions or to exercise command over matters that touch them directly, such as the reservation school system. Strikingly, these Fox elicit from neighboring Whites many of the judgments applied to the Short Grass Cree.

Whites regard the Fox as lacking ambition, as persons who are unhealthily dependent on White economic support but are at the same time only marginally part of the larger society. Gearing attributes this to the "estrangement" of Whites from Indians: Whites are largely ignorant of Fox Indian ways and are thus unable to relate to Indians as whole persons.

In all these cases, as in Short Grass, it appears that most Indians and Whites are unaware of much that they communicate to one another about themselves, and that this ignorance has profound effects on perpetuating the structure of the community.

I have mentioned that Whites consider Indians to be profane persons. One aspect of such profanation, akin to a similar aspect of the plight of stigmatized individuals generally, is that it pervades the whole of Indian social character in the thought of Whites. It seems that when a person possesses a serious disfigurement of self it will contaminate the rest of his social self, disqualifying him thoroughly from normal interaction. The mark of a stigmatized person is that his failing is assumed in all situations. A man with a known prison record, for example, is thought incapable of conventional family living, holding down a bonded job, or acting as an unblemished and trustworthy citizen.

This, of course, is what has happened to Indians in Short Grass. Whites who have seen what they label as Indian misbehavior in town always expect the worst and assume that similar sorts of things occur on the reserve. For example, many Whites who have never visited the reserve are sure that its residents are indiscriminately promiscuous. "There's a lot of interbreeding up there, if you know what I mean," one man said with a wink. A ranch wife warned me at the beginning of my fieldwork, "If I was you, I'd stay away from them Indian girls; otherwise you'll have to hang a sign around your waist saying 'Closed For Repairs.'" Most Whites, who are unaware of Indian marriage patterns and the cultural continuity these represent but who know that Indians are not "churched," take this as evidence that Indians do not really know the institution of marriage at all. They insist that Indian men and women mate more or less randomly, and do not have "normal" family lives. In this and in every other respect, Indians fall short in the eyes of their "civilized" neighbors.

Pluralistic Ignorance

In an important article on the role of ignorance in the workings of society, Louis Schneider (1962) has drawn together some diverse views from both the functional and organic schools of social thought. He is primarily concerned with the "eufunctional" effects of ignorance on social institutions, but his observations are relevant to the question of social stability in Short Grass.

Just as Whites are ignorant of daily life on the reserve, Indians have little idea of the domestic life of Whites. Friendships between Indian and White individuals are extremely rare—that is, friendships that might provide a flow of information between the two. When Indian men work for White ranchers, they do so outdoors and are not usually invited to eat at the family table. Even when an Indian lives on a ranch, he and his family are provided with their own quarters. Indian women do not work as domestics in White households. And at school, Indian and White children do not play together. Opportunities for Indians to observe and interact with Whites, then, are largely restricted to the pubs, cafes, and other public places; and Indians, in their turn, speculate about private goings-on among Whites. Interestingly, they are as sure as Whites are that members of the other group are sexually promiscuous. One Indian insisted to me that the wife of a nearby rancher entertained a lover whenever her husband was away from home— even though the woman is in her early sixties and weighs over 300 pounds.[3] Similarly, if one believed Indian reports, the number of White prostitutes in town would be a high proportion of the female population indeed.

[3] Speculation about other people's intimate lives seems to be a generally favored pastime in Short Grass. A White rancher who knew that the Hutterite colonies in the region have some sort of communalism confided to me that the Hutterite men and women live in separate houses, and that once a year all the men go to the women's dorm to have sexual intercourse. He supposed the reason for this was that all children would then be born at one time of the year, simplifying both medical arrangements and the celebration of birthdays. I heard other versions of the same story.

To Indians, strictly White spheres of action are mysterious, dark places where vaguely specified but nefarious things go on. All this is to be expected. As Shibutani (1962) has masterfully argued, communal structures such as ethnic groups are closed social worlds, networks of interacting individuals who construct and defend identities within their perceived boundaries. In Short Grass, the Indians' ignorance of White ways of life makes it possible for them to construct fantasy pictures of White impurity. They can thus rescue a degree of self-worth to the extent that they deny it to Whites; and this is made possible by the absence of conflicting information about Whites. Thus ignorance is stabilizing, that is, it averts open conflict. "Knowledge would bring awareness to the previously ignorant that they were being handled in such a fashion as to bring about some end defined as socially necessary or desirable by manipulators or by others" (Schneider, 1962: 505).

The end desired by Whites in Short Grass is that Indians not make extensive demands on White resources, such as money and land. This issue can be quite a real one at times:

Tim McKay wanted to buy some land through the Department of Natural Resources but had uncovered an old map that showed the parcel to be a part of the reserve. He was finally, by secret negotiations, able to get the map declared erroneous. TM says he tried to keep all of this quiet. "That's all I needed, was for them buggers to find out that land was supposed to be theirs."

There was also the case of a White rancher who, with the approval of most of his neighbors, attempted unsuccessfully to have the whole band moved to another reserve. His hope was that the Short Grass reserve land would then become federal grazing land, where he and others might winter their cattle. He even made a trip to Ottawa to speak with higher-ups in the Indian Affairs Branch in support of his proposal, but with no tangible success.[4]

────────

[4] There was another affair, somewhat veiled in intrigue, concerning expansion of the reserve. Land is at a premium in the region, especially ranching land, since ranches require considerably more space than farms. At the time people were moving off their small places on the bench a number of ranches came up for sale, but only one of them was purchased by the IAB for the Indians. It is said that a number of ranchers (and the Cattlemen's Association)

Another manifestation of the apprehensiveness of Whites concerns the possibility of Indians moving to town. A councilman with whom I talked was dead set against this, even though a couple of Indian families had occupied shacks in town for brief periods.

It's just asking for trouble. They don't take care of anything. They got no business here; they got no proper work to do, and would just be here so that they'd be closer to the pubs. We would just have a lot of trouble, there'd be fights, and who knows, maybe there would start to be violence between Indians and Whites, especially between Indians and some of the good-for-nothing Whites already living in town. No, it's better all around that they stay where they belong. We don't want any Indian town on the edge of Short Grass. We got too much invested in keeping Short Grass clean and peaceful.

Similarly, most Whites insist that aid of various forms ought not to be extended to Indians; many, in fact, feel that relief and other forms of "dole" should be discontinued entirely, since these handouts have only had a deleterious effect. A little hardship, they feel, would do the Indians good, teach them to look out for themselves.

In the previous chapter, I discussed an aspect of Indian adaptation to an interior place in the community that has the effect of "cooling out." Insofar as Indians regard the gains they receive in transactions with Whites as real and substantial, they will continue to enter into these transactions. Their attention is diverted from the exploitative nature of their subordinate status in part by their seeing themselves as exploiters of Whites. On the White side of things, ignorance has somewhat different effects. Were Whites to become cognizant of the cultural differences between themselves and Indians—were they to have a more intimate knowledge of reserve life—this knowledge would, in Schneider's terms, "initiate serious self-questioning" (1962: 505). The fact that Whites, in large part through ignorance, are able to maintain an image of Indians as profane persons justifies a special treatment of band members that violates the usual norms governing interpersonal behavior.

_____

got together to block the sale of other ranches to the IAB—land that eventually became the present grazing cooperative. One rancher, whose land had been sold, said to me: "The IAB really missed the boat then. The reserve could have been tripled in size if they'd been able to get that land."

It appears also that there is a kind of perceptual blindness to information about Indians that might alter the Whites' image of them. For example, an elementary school teacher who has a few Indian children in her class said: "I have to keep reminding myself that they don't know English, and that that is the reason they don't seem to respond . . . not that they are stupid or anything." Schneider's observation is pertinent: a person "cognizant of the sociological perspective may seek to ignore it in an attempt to preserve belief" (1962: 505).

Indian "antisocial" behavior may also be regarded as a series of small "blowups," a letting-off of steam. A person who has suffered a loss or who has failed to successfully operate in a role may be permitted to give vent to his anger, to momentarily renounce the system so that things can return to "normal." For example, two young Indian men who were asked to leave a pub (neither was drunk) responded by heaving a 60-pound bale of hay into the hotel lobby. The bale burst near two large electric fans, scattering hay over the place. The Indians had been genuinely and deeply angry; but, with the exception of the hotel owner, the incident was regarded by Whites as a humorous and mischievous prank of little consequence.

Thus it appears that various sorts of protective measures are taken, by both Indians and Whites, to ensure the perpetuation of the status quo in Short Grass. This, it may be noted, is a pervasive aspect of human interaction. When conventional images of social selves are threatened, more is at stake than these selves alone: the entire situation is jeopardized, as well as the social system of which it is a part. In Short Grass, Indians and Whites alike tenaciously hold to their respective images of one another. Both groups shore up the barriers blocking information that might bring about redefinitions of themselves, of the situations in which they interact, and of the society built out of these situations.

Schneider, in criticizing functional and organic social theorists, has brought up the problem of what he calls "transmutation mechanisms." These are the "*precise ways* in which individual purposive actions addressed to limited objects can lead on to uncontemplated social effects" (1962: 500). This, I think, is also the point of Blumer's criticism (1956) of "variable analysis" in modern social science: namely, that it neglects the continuous interpretation by acting individuals of their environment and the formation of plans of action based on meanings imposed on the environment, which in turn result in abstract "social structures." The problem is how one should link situational and institutional analyses of human conduct. How do individuals come to act so that their acts cumulatively bring about or retard institutional and cultural change?

When an Indian fails to show up at a certain place at a certain time, does not pay a debt, or "exploits" some relationship with a White, he establishes for Whites the image of himself as irresponsible and untrustworthy. This sort of image, once formed and validated by action, influences the later behavior of Whites toward Indians. Similarly, when a White performs in a way that Indians would expect from their image of Whites, stability is given to the enduring patterns of interaction that contain these reciprocal images. Cumulatively, the social selves negotiated in daily interaction thus become transmuted into the relatively stable "system" of ethnic stratification in Short Grass.

One incident I encountered illustrates the process very well. Shortly before the yearly Sun Dance, a small group of Indians approached several White ranchers, one at a time, to ask that a cow be donated to the band to provide meat for the ceremonial feast. The Indians felt that since the Sun Dance was intended to bring rain and a general renewal of nature, benefiting everyone, Whites could reasonably be expected to contribute to the ceremony. This had, in fact, been the custom in the old days; but now the Indians were refused. "Why the hell should *I* give *you* an expensive animal?" one rancher protested. Later, an Indian spoke of this response as further proof of the stinginess and uncaring of Whites, remarking that the Indians knew they probably would be refused but had decided to ask anyway. And in all probability the ranchers approached viewed the episode as another, predictable, example of Indian freeloading.

A Complementarity of Moral Affronts

In assessing the status and achievements of culture and personality research, Anthony Wallace has addressed himself to the problem of what is shared by members of societies. He concludes (1961: 37) that "cognitive sharing is not *necessary* for stable social interaction." There are circumstances in which the parties to an interaction need not know what their respective "motives" are; indeed, they may not even know who their opposite numbers are (as in silent trade). People can continue to interact even if they greatly misconstrue one another's real motives: it is only necessary that they consummate one another's instrumental acts. To the extent that persons' actions articulate with one another—that mutual expectations are met—people can engage in repeated interactions without being aware of the larger consequences of their actions.

These observations can be extended to the point of hypothesizing that a certain degree of "ignorance" is actually necessary to the smooth functioning of society. In Wallace's terms (1961: 39–40): "We may now suggest that human societies may characteristically *require* the nonsharing of certain cognitive maps among participants in a variety of institutional arrangements. Many a social subsystem simply will not work if all participants share common knowledge of the system." The functions of cognitive nonsharing, Wallace continues, are to permit a more complex social system than would be possible were it restricted to what people could grasp, and to relieve individuals "from the heavy burden of knowing each other's motivations" (1961: 40).

In Short Grass the respective self-images of Indians and Whites take a dual form in which each appears morally inferior to the other. And each group acts in ways that project this image of inferiority to the other, though largely ignorant of this result of their actions. There is a sort of negative division of symbolic labor: the attainment of a morally defensible self for both Indian and White occurs at the expense of the other, and in an atmosphere in which each represents a moral threat to the other. The failure, or refusal, of Whites to extend assistance of some kind to Indians is taken by them as evidence of their moral superiority, but is taken by Indians as proof of White moral failure. Conversely, sharing among Indians is seen by them as a reflection of their moral worth, whereas Whites see it as evidence of the Indians' greediness and as a cause of their low economic and moral status. There is a complementarity in which Indians and Whites, in doing what they think proper, each offer to the other clear proof of moral deficiency.

This, then, is the nature of the larger "working consensus" in Short Grass. The definition of a given situation is more complex than either Indians or Whites realize, containing contradictory and morally loaded claims about relative personal worth. But these claims do not lead to overt conflict because both groups do not fully comprehend the results of their acts. In essence, a sort of moral standoff is effected.

Society and the Assignment of Moral Worth

In societies that are stratified ethnically or otherwise, it is apparently common for various segments of the society (or community) to make moral evaluations of one another, which are frequently uncomplimentary. This is so in Short Grass, and appears to be so in a wide range of other cases reported by social scientists and other writers. Examples can be found almost anywhere one cares to look—in most of the monographs mentioned at various points in this volume, for instance.

A 1969 collection of reports edited by Frederick Barth (1969), which concerns the boundaries of ethnic groups in diverse societies, contains many illustrations of situations where there is mutual disesteem between groups and mutual reinforcement or validation of this judgment. As an example, Harald Eidheim's paper in that volume, "When Ethnic Identity Is a Social Stigma," describes a Lapp community in northern Norway. The stigmatization of Lapps in this case is much more subtle than that of Indians in Short Grass; indeed, Eidheim claims that an outsider might not even notice ethnic stratification at all. Nevertheless, Lapps find themselves regarded as members of a profane category of persons and make efforts to cover their Lappishness. "In very general terms, one may say that the basis for their dilemma is that in order to achieve the material and social goods they appreciate, and to share the opportunities available in the society, people have to get rid of, or cover up, those characteristics which Norwegians take as signs of Lappishness (Eidheim, 1969: 45). Only in the company of other Lapps do individuals drop this concealment of Lappish identity; when Norwegians are present, they cover up. In other words, there is no shared agreement on the moral value of all participants to interaction in this community.

The phenomenon occurs in contexts other than ethnically mixed ones. The members of various castes in a Himalayan community described by Berreman (1962) are bound up in a similar sort of information game. Low-caste people, who are defined as polluting to higher castes, frequently surmise a great deal about the private lives of their betters, and assert that Brahmins do not always live up to the ritual constraints on their conduct. Though they do not openly say so, lower-caste members take this as proof that the Brahmin claims of moral elevation are overblown. "They are not so much better than us after all," one might put it.

In stratified societies, then, public convention often assigns greater ritual or moral value to persons at the top of the hierarchy. Implicitly, however, those in lower positions may assign themselves greater moral worth, at the expense of their betters. And it further appears that members of each group usually act so as to validate their own ideas about themselves on the one hand and about their moral inferiors on the other. From the outside, all this resembles an impasse, though one of which the participants are largely unaware in any detail. But—and this is important—it seems that such communities can function comparatively smoothly and can achieve relative stability. I have suggested that this stability requires all parties to remain ignorant of the full moral implications of their expressive acts as they validate beliefs about relative moral worth.

I am left with two questions—and no ready answer for them. First, is it inevitable in social life that a sense of moral value can be secured by individuals or groups only at the expense of others? In anthropology, we know that whenever there are social divisions into various kinds of groups there is frequently a mutual lack of esteem; this is true whether the divisions are between clans or lineages, age-grades or villages, tribes or races. What varies is how extremely these beliefs are held, how vigorously the moral worth of others is denied for one's own benefit. But it would seem, for example, that the friendly rivalry between two Sioux military societies and the murderous hatred expressed between Yanomamo villages contain fundamentally similar tendencies: in each case the members of one group contrast themselves with those of another, to their own moral advantage. Does this always hold true?

The second question, equally pressing, is related to the first. At what point do persons whose group membership denies them moral value in the official scheme of things refuse to go along with that scheme? What is it that brings some Indians, American Blacks, or modern women to no longer accept their profane status? (These are all, of course, what we call ascribed statuses, and the possessors of them do not always constitute "groups" in the conventional sense of the word.) In our society many members of groups whose positions have been assigned to them on the arbitrary basis of birth have said, in effect: "No more! No longer will we accept designation as inferior beings!" Their goal, it would seem, is to alter the moral order fundamentally, in the sense that they wish the official scheme of things to affirm that they are the possessors of morally valuable and ritually deserving selves. They have, in other words, made overt their previously hidden claims about themselves. It is not clear what, precisely, triggers this action.

The second question is especially important for Short Grass because its Indians have not yet taken the course of rebellion. On other reservations, a growing number of Indians have done so, insisting, among other things, upon their right to manage their own affairs without government interference. There is more at stake here than a share in the material wealth of industrial society: this, I think, is a less important issue than the public validation of claims to a morally sacred self. In Short Grass, Indians have not yet taken up this moral challenge, but they will certainly do so in time, and the problem is whether or not this can be done without permanently unhappy consequences for either Indian or White.

Bibliography

Bibliography

Ablon, Joan. 1964. Relocated American Indians in the San Francisco Bay Area: Social interaction and Indian identity. Hum. Org. 24: 296–304.

Banton, Michael. 1965. Roles: An introduction to the study of social relations. London: Tavistock.

Barth, Frederick. 1966. Models of social organization. Roy. Anthrop. Inst. Occ. Pap. 23.

——— ed. 1969. Ethnic groups and boundaries. Boston: Little, Brown.

Basso, Keith H. 1970. To give up on words: Silence in Western Apache culture. Sthwest. J. Anthrop. 26: 213–30.

Bateson, Gregory. 1958. Naven. 2d ed. Stanford, Calif.: Stanford Univ. Press.

Bennett, John W. 1968. Risk and rationality: Aspects of behavioral adaptation in an arid-variable habitat. Plns. Anthrop. 8: 1–6.

——— 1969. Northern plainsmen. Chicago: Aldine.

Berreman, Gerald D. 1962. Behind many masks: Ethnography and impression management in a Himalayan village. Soc. Appl. Anthrop. Monogr. 4.

——— 1964. Aleut reference group alienation, mobility, and acculturation. Amer. Anthrop. 66: 231–50.

Bidney, David. 1953. Theoretical anthropology. New York: Columbia Univ. Press.

Blumer, Herbert. 1956. Sociological analysis and the "variable." Amer. Soc. Rev. 21: 683–90.

——— 1962. Society as symbolic interaction. In A. M. Rose, ed., Human behavior and social processes. Boston: Houghton Mifflin.

Braroe, Niels W. 1968. Continuity and change in the development of a pre-literate state. Anthropologica 10: 3–27.

Bruner, Edward M. 1956. Primary group experience and the process of acculturation. Amer. Anthrop. 58: 605–23.

——— 1961. Mandan. In E. Spicer, ed., Perspectives in American Indian culture change. Chicago: Univ. Chicago Press.

Cavan, Sheri. 1966. Liquor license: An ethnography of bar behavior. Chicago: Aldine.

Chance, Norman A. 1965. Acculturation, self-identification, and personality adjustment. Amer. Anthrop. 67: 372–93.

Cooley, Charles H. 1964. Human nature and the social order. New York: Schocken.

Cowie, Isaac. 1911. The company of adventurers. Toronto: William Briggs.

Cushman, Dan. 1953. Stay away, Joe. New York: Viking.

Denig, Edwin T. 1961. Five Indian tribes of the Upper Missouri. Norman, Okla.: Univ. Oklahoma Press.

Denzin, Norman K. 1970. The research act. Chicago: Aldine.

Deutsch, Morton, and R. M. Krauss. 1965. Theories in social psychology. New York: Basic Books.

Diamond, Stanley. 1964. Introduction: The uses of the primitive. *In* S. Diamond, ed., *Primitive views of the world.* New York: Columbia Univ. Press.

Douglas, Mary. 1966. Purity and danger. London: Routledge and Kegan Paul.

Durkheim, Emile. 1957. Elementary forms of religious life. London: Allen and Unwin.

Eidheim, Harald. 1969. When ethnic identity is a social stigma. *In* F. Barth, ed., *Ethnic groups and boundaries.* Boston: Little, Brown.

Ellison, Ralph. 1953. The invisible man. New York: New American Library.

Erickson, Eric H. 1956. The problem of ego identity. J. Amer. Psychoanal. Soc. 4: 58–121.

Ewers, John C. 1958. The Blackfeet. Norman, Okla.: Univ. Oklahoma Press.

Firth, Raymond. 1956. Elements of social organization (rev. ed.). London: Watts.

French, David. 1961. Wasco-Wishram. *In* E. H. Spicer, ed., *Perspectives on American Indian culture change.* Chicago: Univ. Chicago Press.

Gearing, Frederic O. 1970. The face of the Fox. Chicago: Aldine.

Glaser, Nathan, and D. P. Moynihan. 1963. Beyond the melting pot: The Negroes, Puerto Ricans, Jews, Italians, and Irish of New York City. Cambridge, Mass.: M.I.T. Press.

Gluckman, Max, ed. 1962. Essays on the ritual of social relations. Manchester, Eng.: Manchester Univ. Press.

——— 1965. Politics, law, and ritual in tribal society. Chicago: Aldine.

Goffman, Erving. 1956. On the nature of deference and demeanor. Amer. Anthrop. 58: 473–502.

——— 1959. The presentation of self in everyday life. New York: Doubleday Anchor Books.

——— 1961. Encounters: Two studies in the sociology of interaction. Indianapolis: Bobbs-Merrill.

——— 1962. On cooling the mark out. *In* A. M. Rose, ed., *Human behavior and social processes.* Boston: Houghton Mifflin.

——— 1963a. Behavior in public places: Notes on the social organization of gatherings. New York: Free Press.

——— 1963b. Stigma: Notes on the management of spoiled identity. Englewood Cliffs, N.J.: Prentice-Hall.

Goodenough, Ward H. 1963. Cooperation in change. New York: Russell Sage Foundation.

Graves, Theodore D. 1967. Acculturation, access and alcoholism in a tri-ethnic community. Amer. Anthrop. 69: 306–21.

Hallowell, A. Irving. 1955. Culture and experience. Philadelphia: Univ. Pennsylvania Press.

Haydon, Alfred L. 1910. The riders of the plains. Chicago.

Hoebel, E. Adamson. 1954. The law of primitive man. Cambridge, Mass.: Harvard Univ. Press.

Honigman, John J., and I. Honigman. 1944. Drinking in an Indian-White community. Quart. J. Stud. Alcohol 5: 575–619.

Howard, Joseph K. 1952. Strange empire: A narrative of the Northwest. New York: Morrow.

Hughes, Charles, 1957. Reference-group concepts in the study of a changing Eskimo culture. Proceedings of the 1957 Annual Spring Meetings of the American Ethnological Society. Seattle: Univ. Washington Press.

Innis, Harold A. 1962. The fur trade in Canada (rev. ed.). New Haven: Yale Univ. Press.

Jarvie, I. C. 1964. The revolution in anthropology. London: Routledge and Kegan Paul.

Jefferson, Robert. 1929. Fifty years on the Saskatchewan. Canad. N.W. Hist. Soc. Publ., Vol. 1, No. 5.

Jenness, Diamond. 1932. The Indians of Canada. Dept. Mines, Nat. Mus. Canad., Anthrop. Ser. 15.

Jessor, Robert, et al. 1968. Society, personality, and deviant behavior. New York: Holt, Rinehart, & Winston.

Jorgensen, Joseph G. 1971. Indians in the metropolis. *In* J. O. Waddell and O. M. Watson, eds., *The American Indian in urban society.* Boston: Little, Brown.

Kane, Paul. 1968. Wanderings of an artist among the Indians of North America. Rutland, Vt.: Tuttle.

Kinch, John W. 1963. A formalized theory of self-concept. Amer. J. Soc. 68: 481–86.

Kuhn, Manfred H. 1964. Major trends in symbolic interaction theory in the past twenty-five years. Soc. Quart. 5: 61–84.

Leach, Edmund R. 1965. Political systems of highland Burma. Boston: Beacon.

Lee, Dorothy. 1959. Freedom and culture. Englewood Cliffs, N.J.: Prentice-Hall.

Lemert, Edwin M. 1954. Alcohol and the Northwest Coast Indians. Univ. Calif. Publ. Cult. & Soc. 2: 303–406.

Linton, Ralph, ed. 1940. Acculturation in seven American Indian tribes. New York: Appleton-Century.

Llewellyn, Karl N., and E. Adamson Hoebel. 1941. The Cheyenne way. Norman, Okla.: Univ. Oklahoma Press.

Lyman, Stanford, and M. B. Scott. 1970. A sociology of the absurd. New York: Appleton-Century-Crofts.

Lynd, Helen M. 1958. On shame and the search for identity. New York: Harcourt, Brace.

McCall, George J., and J. L. Simmons. 1966. Identities and interactions: An examination of human associations in everyday life. New York: Free Press.

McFee, Malcom. 1968. The 150% man: A product of Blackfoot acculturation. Amer. Anthrop. 70: 1096–1107.

McHugh, Peter. 1968. Defining the situation: The organization of meaning in social interaction. Indianapolis: Bobbs-Merrill.

Malinowski, Bronislaw. 1922. Argonauts of the Western Pacific. London: Dutton.

Mandelbaum, David G. 1940. The Plains Cree. Anthrop. Paps. Amer. Mus. Nat. Hist., Vol. 37, Pt. 2.

Mead, George H. 1934. Mind, self, and society. Chicago: Univ. Chicago Press.

Mead, Margaret. 1932. The changing culture of an Indian tribe. New York, Columbia Univ. Press.

Meltzer, Bernard N. 1967. Mead's social psychology. *In* J. G. Manis and B. N. Meltzer, eds., *Symbolic interaction*. Boston: Allyn and Bacon.

Messinger, Sheldon, H. Sampson, and R. D. Towne. 1962. Life as theater: Some notes on the dramaturgic approach to social reality. Sociometry 25: 98–110.

Murphy, Robert F. 1964a. Social distance and the veil. Amer. Anthrop. 66: 1257–74.

———— 1964b. Social change and acculturation. Trans. N.Y. Acad. Sci., Ser. 2, 26: 845–54.

Norbeck, Fred. 1963. African rituals of conflict. Amer. Anthrop. 65: 1257–79.

Oliver, S. 1962. Ecology and cultural continuity as contributing factors in the social organization of Plains Indians. Univ. Calif. Publ. Amer. Archaeol. & Ethnol., Vol. 48, No. 1.

Opler, Marvin K., ed. 1959. Culture and mental health: Cross-cultural studies. New York: Macmillan.

Opler, Morris E. 1964. The human being in culture theory. Amer. Anthrop. 66: 507–28.

Paget, Amelia. 1909. My people of the plains. Toronto: Ryerson.

Parker, Seymour. 1964. Ethnic identity and acculturation in two Eskimo villages. Amer. Anthrop. 66: 325–40.

Pettitt, George A. 1946. Primitive education in North America. Univ. Calif. Publ. Amer. Archaeol. & Ethnol., Vol. 43, No. 1.

Piers, George, and M. R. Singer. 1953. Shame and guilt. Chicago: Thomas.

Redfield, Robert. 1953. The primitive world and its transformations. Ithaca, N.Y.: Cornell Univ. Press.

Roe, Frank G. 1951. The native American buffalo. Toronto: Univ. Toronto Press.

Rose, Arnold M. 1962. A systematic summary of symbolic interaction theory. *In* A. M. Rose, ed., *Human behavior and social processes*. Boston: Houghton Mifflin.

Schneider, Louis. 1962. The role of the category of ignorance in sociological theory: An exploratory formulation. Amer. Soc. Rev. 27: 492–508.

Secoy, Frank R. 1953. Changing military patterns on the Great Plains, 17th century through early 19th century. Monogr. Amer. Ethnol. Soc. 21.

Sharp, Paul F. 1955. Whoop-up country: The Canadian-American West, 1865–1885. Minneapolis: Univ. Minnesota Press.

Shibutani, Tamotsu. 1962. Reference groups and social control. *In* A. M. Rose, ed., *Human behavior and social processes*. Boston: Houghton Mifflin.

Simmel, Georg. 1950. The sociology of Georg Simmel (K. H. Wolff, ed.). Glencoe, Ill.: Free Press.

Skinner, Allison. 1914. Political organizations, cults, and ceremonies of the Plains Cree. Anthrop. Paps. Amer. Mus. Nat. Hist., Vol. 11, Part 6.

——— 1919. The Sun Dance of the Plains Cree. Anthrop. Paps. Amer. Mus. Nat. Hist., Vol. 16, Pt. 4.

Social Science Research Council. 1954. Acculturation: An exploratory formulation (Summer Seminar on Acculturation, 1953). Amer. Anthrop. 56: 973–1002.

Spicer, Edward H., ed. 1961. Perspectives in American Indian culture change. Chicago: Univ. Chicago Press.

Spindler, George, and W. Goldschmidt. 1952. Experimental design in the study of culture change. Sthwest. J. Anthrop. 8: 68–83.

Spindler, George, and L. Spindler. 1965. The instrumental activities inventory: A technique for the study of the psychology of acculturation. Sthwest. J. Anthrop. 21: 1–23.

Stegner, Wallace. 1955. Wolf willow. New York: Viking.

Steward, Julian, and R. F. Murphy. 1956. Tappers and trappers: Parallel processes in acculturation. Econ. Devel. & Cult. Change 4: 335–55.

Stone, Gregory P. 1962. Appearance and the self. *In* A. M. Rose, ed., *Human behavior and social processes*. Boston: Houghton Mifflin.

Strauss, Anselm. 1959. Mirrors and masks. Glencoe, Ill.: Free Press.

Thomas, William I. 1924. The unadjusted girl. Boston: Little, Brown.

Turner, Ralph H. 1962. Role-taking: Process versus conformity. *In* A. M.

Rose, ed., *Human behavior and social processes.* Boston: Houghton Mifflin.

Turner, Victor W. 1962. Three symbols of *passage* in Ndembu circumcision ritual: An interpretation. *In* M. Gluckman, ed., *Essays on the ritual of social relations.* Manchester, Eng.: Univ. Manchester Press.

———— 1968. The drums of affliction. London: Oxford Univ. Press.

Wallace, Anthony F. C. 1961. Culture and personality. New York: Random House.

Wax, Rosalie H. 1971. Doing fieldwork. Chicago: Univ. Chicago Press.

West, James. 1945. Plainville, U.S.A. New York: Columbia Univ. Press.

Wissler, Clark. 1936. Changes in population profiles among the Northern Plains Indians. Anthrop. Paps. Amer. Mus. Nat. Hist. Vol. 36, Pt. 1.

Zetterberg, Hans L. 1966. The secret ranking. J. Marr. & Fam. 28: 134–42.

Index

Index